A Canadian Conversation Book

English in Everyday Life

Second Edition

A Canadian Conversation Book

English in Everyday Life

Second Edition

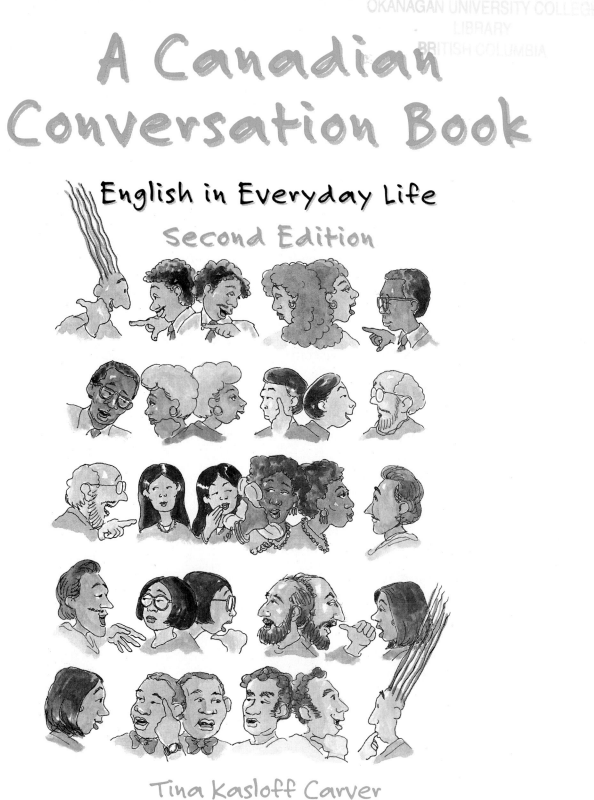

Tina Kasloff Carver
Sandra Douglas Fotinos
Clarice Cooper

Prentice Hall Allyn and Bacon Canada
Scarborough, Ontario

Canadian Cataloguing in Publication Data

Carver, Tina Kasloff, 1944–
    A Canadian conversation book: English in everyday life.
2nd ed.
ISBN 0-13-599275-3

1. English language – Textbooks for second language learners.* 2. English language –
Conversation and phrase books. I. Fotinos, Sandra Douglas, 1940–   . II. Cooper, Clarice,
1932–   . III. Title.

PE1131.C37 1997   428.3'4   C96-931964-9

© 1997 Prentice-Hall Canada Inc., Scarborough, Ontario
A Division of Simon & Schuster/A Viacom Company

Prentice-Hall, Inc., Upper Saddle River, New Jersey
Prentice-Hall International (UK) Limited, London
Prentice-Hall of Australia, Pyt. Limited, Sydney
Prentice-Hall Hispanoamericana, S.A., Mexico City
Prentice-Hall of India Private Limited, New Delhi
Pretice-Hall of Japan, Inc., Tokyo
Simon & Schuster Southeast Asia Private Limited, Singapore
Editora Prentice-Hall do Brasil, Ltda., Rio de Janeiro

ISBN 0-13-599275-3

Acquisitions Editor: Cliff Newman
Developmental Editor: Marta Tomins
Production Editor: Susan James
Production Coordinator: Julie Preston
Cover design: Laura Ierardi, Mary Opper
Interior Design: Noël Vreeland Carter
Art: Andrew Lange
Page Layout: Jack Steiner

Original English Language edition published by Prentice-Hall, Inc., Englewood Cliffs, New Jersey
Copyright © 1991, 1988, 1984, 1980, 1976.

1 2 3 4 5   01 00 99 98 97

Printed and bound in the U.S.A.

Visit the Prentice Hall Canada Web site! Send us your comments, browse our catalogues, and more.
www.phcanada.com Or reach us through e-mail at phabinfo_pubcanada@prenhall.com

CONTENTS

UNIT 1: WELCOME TO CLASS!   1

LESSON	COMPETENCY OBJECTIVES	PAGE
Welcome to Class!	• identify self and others • request and give information	2
What Is Your Nationality?		4
Countries	• locate geographical areas	5
Numbers	• learn cardinal numbers • count	7
Journal	• express basic personal information and numbers in written form	8
Clothing and Colours	• identify articles of clothing and colours	9
Pairs of Clothing	• identify pairs of clothing	10
What Are They Wearing?	• identify items of clothing	
What Colour Are Your Clothes?	• learn colours	11
Family Tree	• learn family relationships	12
Families	• identify immediate and extended family relationships	13
Review		16

UNIT 2: EVERYDAY LIFE 17

UNIT 3: THE CALENDAR 29

UNIT 4: FOOD

UNIT 5: HOMES   69

UNIT 6: SHOPPING 89

UNIT 7: COMMUNITY 113

UNIT 8: WORK   137

UNIT 9: HEALTH   159

UNIT 10: LEISURE   179

FOREWORD

The second edition of A CANADIAN CONVERSATION BOOK comes three years after the writing of the first. During these years, the field of ESL has changed greatly, but what students need to improve their skills in speaking English has remained the same. Students now, as then, need thought-provoking materials that will be of use to them in their daily lives. Students learn conversation skills best when the learning integrates their own experiences and interests.

We have incorporated the results of our experiences over the past few years in this revision. Although the physical appearance is different—the colour, the art, the page composition—the philosophy remains the same. We have endeavoured to bring to both student and teacher a plethora of topics and experiential material for study and practice. The materials are all student-centred. Although we have updated the methodology, changed much of the format and organization and added colour as a pedagogical device, the basis for the text remains the same. We have developed a high frequency lexis within the context of everyday topics for low level students. As in earlier editions, the organization of the text provides for picking and choosing; the book is not spiralled in difficulty. We are providing a wide variety of springboards for teachers to design their curriculum according to the specific needs of their class. No two classes have the same needs—we have provided for that with a wide diversity of flexible and adaptable materials.

This second edition offers a special new feature—a modified picture dictionary base updated from the most successful pages of the previous editions. It also offers more directed activities and more specific instructions. We have carefully heeded the suggestions of our reviewers as well as the advice of teachers and students over the years.

We hope you will enjoy using A CANADIAN CONVERSATION BOOK, Second Edition, and that it will make your conversation class a meaningful, enjoyable, and memorable learning experience for students and teacher alike.

ACKNOWLEDGMENTS

To the very supportive editorial staff at Prentice Hall Canada Inc. Many thanks for your guidance and assistance.

To the many students past, present and future who I have had the privilege to meet. Your courage and unlimited wealth of life experiences have taught me as much as I hope I have taught you.

To Mickey and our wonderful family for your patience and moral support.

Clarice Cooper

NOTES TO THE TEACHER

These notes are provided as springboards for your own creativity and initiative. Our intention in writing **A CANADIAN CONVERSATION BOOK** was to provide a wide variety of vocabulary and student-centred learning activities for you to use within your own style and that of your beginning and low intermediate students.

Equally important is creating an atmosphere of shared learning in which students' differences are valued and their life experiences are appreciated. Learning a foreign language is perhaps the most threatening of all disciplines yet among the most rewarding. In the conversation class, students need to feel the class is a partnership—one between teacher and student as well as between student and student.

THE FIRST CLASS

The most important goal on the first day of class is to set a supportive, non-threatening learning environment. The room should be appealing; if possible, provide a way of relaxation for the students (who may be quite anxious) such as playing music when they arrive and/or offering coffee and tea and a snack. This will prove to be a worthwhile investment of time and thought.

- Provide name tags for all students (either just first names or both first and last). Wear one yourself.

- Spend time talking with students before even tackling the first page of the text. (Perhaps you don't even want to use the text during the first class; instead, have an informal, ice breaking session. Use the material of the text but without the text itself.)

- Use yourself as a model. Try to scout any students who may know a little more and use them as models too.

- Introduce yourself, speaking slowly. Ask, **"What's your name?"** If a student doesn't understand, use another student as a model, or ask yourself and answer it as a model. Write the questions on the board to help students who may recognize written words but not be able to understand what you are saying. As the semester proceeds, both you and your students will learn to understand each other's speech. In the meantime, provide written reinforcement to reduce anxiety.

There is a "mascot" throughout the book. Sometimes he is sitting on the vocabulary boxes, sometimes he is integrated into the drawings. You and the class may want to <u>name</u> the mascot during the first session. This could be an enjoyable "**Name Game.**" Ask the class to suggest names for him. List the names on the board. Then have the class vote on the names and give him the name the students select.

VOCABULARY

Although the lessons in **A CANADIAN CONVERSATION BOOK** are designed for use either sequentially or in random order, the words are only listed once—the first time they appear. Keep this in mind if you are not using the book from beginning to end. Every lesson has at least one vocabulary box. The list in the box is *not* exhaustive, but it does give the basic vocabulary for the lesson. Although words are not repeated in the subsequent boxes, the *items* are found repeatedly throughout the text in the illustrations. For example, the word **shirt** appears first in the lesson on **CLOTHING** on page 9 in UNIT 1. The word does not appear alone in the vocabulary box in the **MEN'S CLOTHING STORE** lesson, but a shirt appears in the *illustration* on page 98. This device can serve as a review.

We have suggested several ways to present the vocabulary in the **Teacher's Manual**. Ultimately, the best methods depend upon your own style of teaching and the students' style of learning. You may want to discuss the illustration first, using the text or the transparency. This allows students to utilize what they know already and lets you assess the class' level of vocabulary proficiency. It also gives an immediate context for the vocabulary. Alternatively, you can simply point to each illustration and ask for the words. This way students associate the illustration with the English word. Combine methods for variety. Any method loses its effectiveness if used over and over again.

Modelling the words for pronunciation is useful for students so they can *hear* how to say the word in English along with *seeing* the illustration and the *written* word. Although sometimes it is difficult for you to hear all the pronunciations, choral repetition will give all students an opportunity to verbalize the words they are learning. Be sure students understand all the words. Sometimes native language translation is appropriate; that is your judgment call!

Note Taking

Suggest that students buy a notebook. Have students divide the notebook into four sections: **Vocabulary, Journal, Community Information, Activities**. When new words are generated in the classroom from discussion or from activities, students should record the words and information in the **Vocabulary** section of their notebooks. Write new words on the board for students to record more easily. The **Journal** section can be used for additional Journal writing. The **Community Information** section should be a place to note valuable information about the students' communities. The **Activities** section should be used for any activities the class does in class or at home. There are specific suggestions in the **Teacher's Manual** as to how and when to use the notebook.

GRAMMAR

Grammar is not treated at all in the student text. In the **Teacher's Manual**, we have made reference to grammar chunks where necessary for clarification. You might want to teach and/or review a particular construction for an activity before or after the activity. The emphasis should be on conversation and communication, not grammatical accuracy.

CORRECTIONS

We are often asked how to handle corrections in the conversation class. Use your own best judgment. Too much correction inhibits students' ability to think coherently and works contrary to practising coherent conversation skills. On the other hand, teachers should aim to strike a balance, teaching syntax as well as pronunciation at opportune times. Make a mental note of the errors students are making. It is usually not helpful to interrupt the flow of students' conversations, but to correct errors at the appropriate time later in class, without referring to any specific students.

GROUPING

Pairing partners can be done in a variety of ways. The easiest way is to have students seated next to each other be partners. However, since an objective of the partner activities is for students to get to know one another, having a variety of partners is essential. Pairing students in different ways maintains students' attention, moves them around the room, and helps them to learn each other's names.

Suggestion:

- Count the students in the class; then divide them in half by left side/right side or front/back.

- Hand out slips of paper to one half of the students.

- Ask them to write their whole names on the paper and fold the paper.

- Collect all the folded papers, then walk through the other half of the class. Have each student pick one folded paper.

- When all the papers are handed out, instruct the students with the papers to find their partners and sit down together.

- Depending on the class (and your own teaching style), you may prefer an open free-for-all with everyone walking around at once, calling out names, or a more structured pairing in which one student at a time reads the name on his or her paper, the student named raises his or her hand, and the two then sit together.

This method of pairing can be used again and again, dividing the class in different ways to assure that students have many different partners and get to know everyone in the class by name.

Partners should always ask each other for their names; there is a place in each **Partner Activity** for students to write their **Partner's name**.

For some activities, larger groups of students are preferable. Again, grouping students can be done in a variety of ways.

Suggestion:

- Have students count off numbers, (1-4, 1-5, 1-6, etc.), then join the group that has their number.

- To practise vocabulary, you may replace numbers with items from the current vocabulary list—colours, fruits, vegetables, flowers, seasons, etc.

- List the group names on the board (for example, with colours, Red, Black, Yellow, Green, etc.), then assign each student a colour and have students form groups, according to their assigned colour.

After students get to know each other, informal methods of pairing or grouping usually work best. Sometimes you can let students choose a partner or set up their own groups. For other activities, depending on the subject matter, you may want to deliberately mix gender, ages, language groups, occupations, or opinions. Try to avoid cliques sitting together. Remind students that the only way to develop conversational fluency in English is to practise in *English*.

PARTNER ACTIVITIES

Partner activities give students non-threatening, one-on-one opportunities to interact on a personal level. They are the only activities in which every student in the class has to do 50% of the talking and has to listen on a one-on-one basis. We have included five types of partner activities: *Games, Interviews, Journals,* and *Role Plays*.

Games

There are two types of partner games: **Memory games (What do you remember?/ Same or different?/Vocabulary Challenges)** and **Mime** games. Always do a "dry run" with the class to make sure that students understand the task.

What do you remember?

- Divide the class into pairs.

- Have the class look at the illustration. Discuss how to remember the details of the illustration as they are looking at it. (How many people, what are the colours, what season is it, what activities do you see, etc.)

- Then have the students close their texts and turn to the <u>Activities</u> section of their notebooks.

- Have the pairs work together, brainstorming everything they remember about the illustration. Have each pair make one list and number each item so that it will be easy to count how many items they listed.

- When students have finished, have different pairs dictate to you the things they remember as you write them on the board. Or have one of the partners write the list on the board. Give several students the opportunity to do this.

- Open the texts or show the transparency. Look at the illustration together.

- Draw a line under the last item you have written and have students dictate additional items as you write them on the board.

- Point out new vocabulary for students to add to the <u>Vocabulary</u> section of their notebooks.

Same or Different?

- Divide the class into pairs.

- Have students study the illustrations they are going to compare.

- Instruct the pairs to make one list of similarities and differences in the illustrations.

- Remind students to number each item so it will be easy to count how many items they listed.

- While students are working, write two horizontal headings: SAME and DIFFERENT.

- When students have finished their lists, call on several pairs to dictate their list as you write on the board.

- Open the texts or show the transparencies. Look at the illustrations together.

- Draw a line under the last item listed. Have students dictate additional items as you write them on the board.

- Point out new vocabulary for students to add to the <u>Vocabulary</u> section of their notebooks.

Mimes:

Sometimes students are asked to act out words or actions with a partner. Demonstrate the activity for the students first so they understand what to do. As the class is doing the activity, circulate; help as needed.

Vocabulary Challenges

- Divide the class into pairs.

- Books must be closed. "Challenge" the pairs of students to make a list of as many vocabulary words and phrases as they remember from the lesson. Have them number the words as they write. Give them a time limit for completing the list.

- When the time is up, ask how many words and phrases each pair had.

- Have a pair read their entire list. Copy it on the board. Star the words that are not from the lesson. Have the class check off the words they have on their lists.

- Have another pair read only the words they have that aren't on the board. List the new words on the board. Star the new words.

- Have the class check off the words they have that are on the board.

- Have another pair read new words from their list. List the new words on the board. Have the class check off any new words.

- Ask which other pair has new words. Add the words to the list.

- Ask which pair had the most new words. They "win" the challenge!

Interviews

It is important, especially during the first days of class, for the students to understand how to conduct these interviews. The teacher's role is to model pronunciation, facilitate understanding of vocabulary and questions, and provide possible answers. For modelling, use a student who will catch on quickly; be careful not to use the same student all the time. Or, if it is more appropriate, model both roles yourself. Write the question and answer on the board so that students can see the questions and answers as well as hear them.

- Practise the interview questions with the students. Be sure they understand the questions and the vocabulary. Supply any additional words needed.

- Divide the class into pairs.

- Have students interview their partners. Circulate; help as needed.

- After partners conduct their interviews, have several pairs present their interviews to the class. Either have them present all questions or have different pairs of partners present one question each. Alternatively, have them share what they have learned about each other with another pair of students.

- Write new vocabulary generated from the interviews on the board. Have students copy the new words in the Vocabulary section of their notebooks.

- Use the students' responses to the interviews for further discussions that may be of interest to the class.

Journals

The journal entries give students a chance to use the vocabulary and phrases they have learned in writing reinforcement activities. Journals should be done as an interactive activity.

- Discuss the topic with the students before they write anything.

- Model and practise the questions provided at the top of the page. Add your own questions if appropriate.

- Divide the class into pairs.

- Have partners ask each other the questions. Circulate; help as needed.

- Have students do their individual journal writing in class or at home.

- Have students proofread their journals.

- Instruct partners to read their journals to each other; encourage them to ask questions and make comments.

- If there is time, have several students read their journals to the class.

- Alternatively, read several journals to the class and have students guess who wrote them.

- Have one or two students put their journal entries on the board. Write the skeleton paragraph as it appears in the text. Either you or the student can fill in the blanks. Have students read what they wrote on the board, or you can read it as a model. Discuss new vocabulary and new ideas.

- Take advantage of any additional topics or information that may emerge to continue conversations and exchanges of information.

- Students can keep more journal pages in the <u>Journal</u> section of their notebooks. Provide guidance for the topics and do light corrections. The object of journal pages is for students to have practice writing fluently in English and expressing their thoughts and emotions. Too much correction will inhibit this goal.

Role Plays

Before students do role playing for the first time, do a sample role play using yourself and another student. This will provide a model for students when they are working independently.

- Divide the class into pairs.

- List the vocabulary needed on the board. Leave the vocabulary on the board as a reference for students when they are working with their partners.

- Students should write the conversation and practise reading their "scripts" with the "read and look up" technique. *(Have the students scan the line and remember it as well as they can; then have them look at the other person and SAY the line without READING it—even beginners can perfect this technique. It helps with the appropriate eye contact and body language required in English.)*

- Have several pairs demonstrate their role plays—with simple props, if appropriate.

- Encourage the pairs to come to the front of the room or sit in the middle of the circle rather than remain at their desks.

- For classes with shy students, an alternative to a traditional role play is a puppet show. Make hand puppets from small paper bags. Cover a table with a sheet for a stage. This activity can be simple or elaborate.

GROUP ACTIVITIES

Group activities give students a feeling of belonging and a feeling of being a part of the group's success. These activities allow students to get to know one another and to cooperate within the framework of different tasks. Many of the activities are cooperative; they require each member of the group to contribute something. While the groups are working, you can move from group to group as a facilitator to be sure students understand their task. After the groups do the activity, there should be a reporting back to the class as a whole so that there can be summation and conclusions can be drawn. We have included seven types of group activities: *Conversation Squares, Discussions, Gossip Games, Problem Posing/Solving, Surveys, Vocabulary Challenges* and *What's the Story?*

Conversation Squares

- Have the students help you create the question they will need to ask for each square.

- Write the questions on the board.

- Construct boxes on the board similar to the ones in the text.

- Choose two students. Use yourself as Number 1.

- Put the three names on the top of the boxes as indicated in the text.

- Ask and answer the questions for your box; write in your responses.

- Ask your partners the questions. Write in their responses.

- Then ask the class the questions for more practice.

- Have groups of three do the activity.

- When all students have finished, ask different groups single questions from the conversation squares. Put new vocabulary on the board for students to write in the **<u>Vocabulary</u>** section of their notebooks.

Discussions

These activities consist of guided questions. Each group should appoint a *leader* to ask the questions and a *recorder* to record the answers. That way, when called upon to recite, students can feel confident in their replies because the answers are written down . Real learning in these activities goes on within the group's dynamic. Reporting back is a way to summarize. Students shouldn't feel intimidated by the reporting back part of the activity. Writing answers usually eliminates this anxiety.

During the reporting back stage, note new vocabulary; write it on the board and have students write the new words in the **Vocabulary** section of their notebooks.

Gossip!

This is a variation of the "Gossip" or "Telephone" game. It has two objectives: to practise new vocabulary in context without visual cues and to demonstrate how information is lost in the process of retelling. A **"Secret"** for each game is included on page 226 of the **Appendix**.

- Divide the class into large groups, or do this activity with the whole class, if your class is small.

- Use the illustration on the text's cover to explain the game. Start on the top left with the mascot. End on the bottom right with the mascot.

- Have the *leader* from each group read the **Secret** silently several times. All other students should have their books closed.

- Have the leaders close their books and quietly whisper the **Secret** to the student next to them. Those students quietly whisper it to the next, and so on. Be sure to explain the words "whisper" and "secret."

- When all students have heard the secret, have the last student of each group report the information to the class, either orally or in written form on the board.

- Have everyone read the **Secret** together to see what information was lost and changed.

Problem Posing/Problem Solving

- Divide the class into small groups.

- Do a practice problem posing/solving example with the class as a whole.

- Have each group choose a recorder and a leader. Each student should participate in some way.

- Before students begin, be sure that they understand the goal of the activity and that they have adequate vocabulary and grammar to do the work.

- Have students think about what is happening in the illustration and formulate a question about it (pose the problem). Remind the leader to ask the questions.

- Then have them think through (analyze) the problem and make a group decision as to what to do (solve the problem). This will take thought, negotiation, resolution, and consensus.

- To summarize, have each recorder report back to the class.

- Draw class conclusions, even if there is diversity of opinion and no real resolution.

Surveys

This activity gives students the opportunity to express their own opinions and preferences, and check their accuracy in listening to and recording answers.

- Model the questions; have students repeat; check pronunciation.

- Be sure students understand all the vocabulary and the objective of the activity before the activity starts.

- Have students check off their own answers in the appropriate column.

- Divide the class into groups of seven to ten. If your class is small, do the activity with the whole class.

- Encourage the students to get up and walk around their group asking questions. Remind them that each student should ask everyone in the group all the questions and check the appropriate column for every answer.

- Set a time limit. Tell students to sit down when they finish and count their results. Remind them to include their own answers in the count.

- Have students report their results to their group. If other members of the group have different numbers, have them figure out who is right.

- While groups are working, copy the chart on the board.

- When groups are sure of their numbers, have them report their results. Fill in the columns on the board and have students draw conclusions about the class.

- Point out new words and have students write them in the **Vocabulary** section of their notebooks.

Vocabulary Challenges

This activity is similar to the *Vocabulary Challenges* as described in the *Memory Games* section of **PARTNER ACTIVITIES**.

What's the Story?

The goal of this activity is to have students look at an illustration (which tells a story), use their imaginations and the vocabulary they know to create their own story. These activities are cooperative learning activities. Each student should contribute one, two, or three lines. The story should be complete and make sense.

- Divide the class into groups.

- Have each group select a *recorder* to write everyone's lines.

- Encourage students to help each other. Be sure that even the shy students participate by contributing their lines.

- After the stories are written, all groups should listen to their recorder read the story. They should all make changes and corrections and "edit" the story before the rest of the class hears it. Have another student (not the recorder) read the story, or have each student read or recite his/her lines.

- Have the class decide which was the best, the most exciting, the saddest, the funniest, etc.

CLASS ACTIVITIES

Class activities provide opportunities for lots of input; this is the advantage of a large class. Many opinions and answers make the class more interesting and exciting. However, if your class functions better in smaller groups, these activities can work as Group Activities also. We have included seven types of class activities: *Community Activities, Cross-Cultural Exchanges, Discussions, Find Someone Who, Strip Stories, Total Physical Response Activities (TPR),* and *Vocabulary Challenges*.

Community Activities

These activities give the class the opportunity to go out into the community and explore, as well as to explore community resources (i.e., the telephone book) in the classroom itself. Students can be sent out individually, in groups, or with partners to gather information requested.

- Review the task before students are asked to do the work independently. Be sure students know the vocabulary and are clear about what they are to do.

- To help prepare students, role play expected scenarios and outcomes. This may avoid pitfalls and panic!

- If possible, accompany the class the first time out. This will give them confidence.

- After the students do the assignment, review it in class.

- Discuss not only the task but what happened—what surprises they had, what reactions they had, how they felt, etc.

- Have student keep important community information in the **Community** section of their notebooks.

Cross-Cultural Exchanges

These activities give the class the opportunity to talk about cultural differences in general as well as about Canadian culture. Students should be encouraged to voice their opinions and confusions about cultures they associate with the English language. Opportunities and interest in this activity will vary with your classes. Wherever possible, compare three or more cultures rather than just two to avoid potential "either/or" interpretations of differences. Encourage intercultural openness and awareness without judgment.

Discussion

Ask the guided questions and choose different students to answer each question. This provides a model for the students. As an alternative approach, you can ask the first question and choose a student to answer. Then have that student ask the second question and choose a student to answer. Continue the pattern. Correct only large errors that impede understanding.

To help structure discussions and teach note taking skills, write a brief heading for each question on the board. Encourage students to do the same in the **Activities** section of their notebooks. List information you gather from the discussions under each heading. Then review your notes and ask the students to review theirs. Draw conclusions together from the notes at the end of the discussion.

Find Someone Who

This activity is similar to the *Survey* activity except in this activity, students are searching for "Yes" answers.

- Review the vocabulary and create the Yes/No questions with the class before they start the activity. Write the questions on the board.

- Give students the grammar constructions in chunks.

- Have the class ask the questions by circulating around the class. If the class is very large, break the class into groups of 10 to 15 and have students do the activity within their group.

- When students have completed their work, have them sit in their seats.

- Review the questions and answers. There should be interesting springboards of conversation that come from the individual answers.

Strip Stories

This visual presentation of little stories gives students the opportunity to discuss the action in the frames and then to write their own captions.

- Have students look at the illustrations and discuss them together.

- Write vocabulary words on the board.

- Ask for suggestions for captions and/or bubbles.

- Write different suggestions on the board. Have students decide which one is best and why.

- Have students write captions in their texts.

- Alternatively, have students create captions individually, in groups or with partners.

Total Physical Response (TPR) Activities

The first Total Physical Response (TPR) activity has illustrations for each of the steps. (See page 6 of the Student Text.) After that, the *instructions* only are in the text.

- Prepare students by giving out slips of paper that they will write something on—an instruction, a favourite month, a favourite food, etc.

- Always model the action before asking students to do it. The object of this activity is for students to associate the action with the words for it. Use exaggerated movements.

- After you do the action, have the class do the action.

- To review, have a student read the actions and have the class follow the instruction. Or have one half of the class read and the other half respond.

- As a written review, dictate the actions and have students write the dictation in the **Activities** section of their notebooks.

Vocabulary Challenges

This activity is similar to the *Vocabulary Challenges* as described in the *Memory Games* section of **PARTNER ACTIVITIES**.

INDIVIDUAL ACTIVITIES

These activities are designed for students to have the opportunity to share their individual perceptions, knowledge, and experiences with the whole class. There are three types of individual activities: *Draw, Speeches,* and *Tell the Class*.

Draw

Students don't have to be artists—nor do you—to do this. A rendition of what is called for is good enough for students to be able to talk about the drawing.

- Give students enough time to complete their drawing.

- Circulate; help as needed, but also scout students who will be able to share a useful drawing—either on the board, a transparency, or photocopies.

- Use your own artwork—the "worse" it is, sometimes, the better. Students are less reluctant to share theirs if yours *isn't* "good"!

- Have students talk about what they drew. Be sure to note new vocabulary words.

Speeches

Students get practice in simple speech writing and recitation with these activities. Give students ample time to prepare. Make the activity VERY structured and help correct as much as you can. Visual aids can help relieve anxiety. Allow students to have note cards, but not to read their speech. Sometimes it is helpful for students to practise with a partner or a small group before addressing the class. There are **Speech** and **Audience Evaluation forms** in the **Appendix**.

Tell the Class

These activities give students the opportunity to be in front of the class and speak without much preparation. With some notes, a little confidence, and a supportive environment, their anxiety levels will be lowered.

TEACHER'S MANUAL

The **Teacher's Manual**, interleaved with actual student text pages, provides the teacher a convenient teaching tool. The format is easy to follow: *Warm Up* activities for each lesson proceed the step-by-step suggestions for all *In the Text* activities. Objectives are clearly stated for each lesson. In addition, there is a wide variety of *Expansion* activities for each lesson. The *To the Teacher* section gives an overview of all activities and objectives.

UNIT 1

Welcome to Class!

WELCOME TO CLASS!

Draw

Draw a picture of yourself.

1. woman	5. single	9. hair	15. eyes	20. glasses
2. man	6. married	10. long	16. brown	21. earrings
3. girl	7. divorced	11. short	17. blue	22. moustache
4. boy	8. widowed	12. curly	18. grey	23. beard
		13. wavy	19. green	
		14. straight		

Write

My name is _____.

1. I am a _____.

2. I am _____.

3. My hair is _____.

4. My eyes are _____.

5. I have _____.

Tell the Class*

Write your first name and your last name on the board. • *Tell the class your name.* • *Show your picture to the class.* • *Describe your picture.*

Partner Activity   Partner's name _____

Introduce yourself to your partner. • *Practise all these ways.*

    A: My name is _____. What's your name? *(or)*
       Hello. I'm _____. What's your name? *(or)*
       Hi. I'm _____. What is your name?

    B: Nice to meet you. My name is _____. *(or)*
       I'm _____. I'm pleased to meet you.

Introduce your partner to the class.

    I'd like you to meet _____. *(or)*
    This is _____.

Group Activity: Introducing Yourself

Work in groups of three or four. • *Write a name tag for yourself.* • *Pronounce the names of each student in your group.* • *Introduce yourself formally to the others in the group and shake hands: Then introduce yourself informally.*

• *Make an alphabetical list of class names.* • *Who has the longest, shortest name?* • *Whose name is the easiest, the most difficult to pronounce?*

Class Discussion: Cultural Differences

Look at the introduction picture below. Do people ever greet each other this way where you come from? Show the class how people greet each other in your native country.

3

WHAT IS YOUR NATIONALITY?

People from many countries live in Canada because it is a nation of immigrants. Here are the names of some of the nations people come from and their nationalities. Notice that many nationalities end in -ese, -ish, or -an. • *Can you fill in the blanks in each list with more nations and nationalities?*

Nation	Nationality	Nation	Nationality
Burma	Burmese	Denmark	Danish
China	Chinese	England	English
Japan	Japanese	Ireland	Irish
Lebanon	Lebanese	Poland	Polish
Portugal	Portuguese	Sweden	Swedish
Vietnam	Vietnamese	Turkey	Turkish
_____	_____	_____	_____
_____	_____	_____	_____
Armenia	Armenian	Chile	Chilean
Brazil	Brazilian	Cuba	Cuban
Canada	Canadian	The Dominican Republic	Dominican
Colombia	Colombian		
Ecuador	Ecuadorian	Germany	German
Egypt	Egyptian	Kenya	Kenyan
Ethiopia	Ethiopian	Korea	Korean
Hungary	Hungarian	Mexico	Mexican
India	Indian	Puerto Rico*	Puerto Rican
Indonesia	Indonesian	Uganda	Ugandan
Iran	Iranian	The United States of America (U.S.A.)	American
Italy	Italian		
Panama	Panamanian		
Russia	Russian	Venezuela	Venezuelan
Tahiti	Tahitian		

Speech: Your Native Country

Prepare a brief speech for your class about your native country. Try to answer these questions in your speech. Add more information too. Practise with a small group before you present your speech to the class. You may use note cards, but do not read your speech.

1. Where is your country (hemisphere, continent, in relation to other countries)?
2. What is its population?
3. What is the capital city?
4. What kind of currency is used?
5. What languages do people speak?
6. What seasons are there? What is the weather like?
7. What kind of government is there?
8. What religions are practised?
9. _____

COUNTRIES

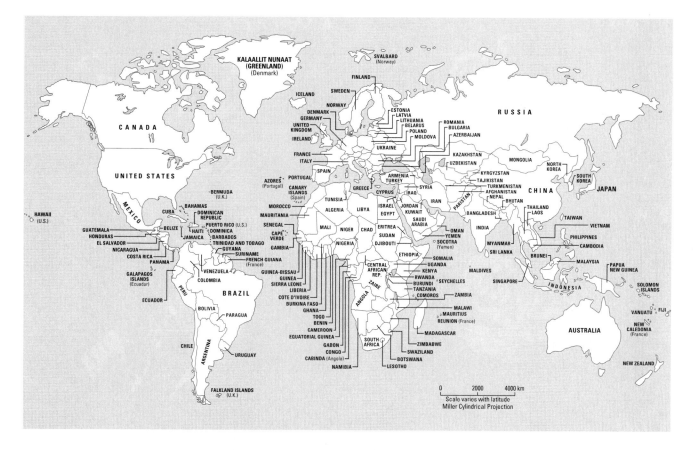

1. world	6. continent	11. Africa
2. map	7. North America	12. Europe
3. country	8. South America	13. Atlantic Ocean
4. island	9. Central America	14. Pacific Ocean
5. city	10. Asia	15. language

Class Activity: Native Countries

Find your native country on the map. • Show your classmates where you are from. Circle the places on your map where all your classmates are from. • Draw a big star where you are now. • Make a list of all the nations and nationalities represented in your class.

Partner Interview ✳

Partner's name _____

Practise these questions with your teacher. • Then ask your partner.

1. What is your name?
2. What country are you from?
3. What city are you from?
4. What continent are you from?
5. Where do you live now?
6. What languages do you speak?

Tell the Class

Tell the class about your partner.

✳ *See Appendix page 225 for Nations/Nationalities.*

Class Game*: *"Where do you want to visit?"*

1. *Think.*

2. *Write.*

3. *Fold.*

4. *Make a pile.*

5. *Open one. Read it to the class.*

6. *Guess who wrote it.*

Tell the Class

Tell the class about the place you want to visit.

* *See Appendix pages 216–221 for Maps.*

6

NUMBERS

0 zero	9 nine	18 eighteen	27 twenty-seven	90 ninety
1 one	10 ten	19 nineteen	28 twenty-eight	100 one hundred
2 two	11 eleven	20 twenty	29 twenty-nine	
3 three	12 twelve	21 twenty-one	30 thirty	
4 four	13 thirteen	22 twenty-two	40 forty	
5 five	14 fourteen	23 twenty-three	50 fifty	
6 six	15 fifteen	24 twenty-four	60 sixty	
7 seven	16 sixteen	25 twenty-five	70 seventy	
8 eight	17 seventeen	26 twenty-six	80 eighty	

Class Activity

Count the men and women in your class. • *Write the correct number and word for each question.* • *Report your answers to the class.*

	MEN	WOMEN
1. How many are there?	_____	_____
2. How many have ?	_____	_____
3. How many are ?	_____	_____
4. How many have blue ?	_____	_____
5. How many have ?	_____	_____
6. How many have ?	_____	_____
7. How many have a ?	_____	_____
TOTALS	_____	_____

Group Activity

Work in groups of four. • *Write the names of all the students in your group.* • *Write what you remember about each student.* • *Compare notes with your group.* • *Read your group's list to the class.*

JOURNAL

Partner Interview

Practise these questions with your teacher. •
Then ask your partner.

1. What is today's date?
2. How many students are in our class?
3. What is your name?
4. What colour is your hair?
5. What colour are your eyes?
6. Are you married or single?
7. Where are you from?
8. What language do you speak?

Partner's name _____

Write

Write about your partner.

Journal

_____
(1)

I am in my English class. There are _____ students
(2)

in my class today. My partner's name is _____.
(3)

She/He has_____ hair and _____ eyes.
(4)   (5)

My partner is _____. She/He is from _____ and
(6)   (7)

speaks _____.
(8)

Tell the Class

Read your journal to the class • *Tell the class about your partner.*

8

CLOTHING AND COLOURS

1. barrette	7. collar	13. raincoat	19. suit
2. bathing suit	8. dress	14. scarf	20. sweater
3. belt	9. handkerchief	15. shirt	21. sweatshirt
4. blouse	10. jacket	16. skirt	22. tie
5. button	11. pocket	17. socks	23. T-shirt
6. coat	12. purse	18. sportscoat	24. zipper

Partner Game: *"What do you remember?"*   **Partner's name** _____

Look at your partner's clothing. • Sit back to back. • Make a list of what your partner is wearing. •
Read your list to your partner. • Don't look at your partner. • Correct your list with your partner.

Class Activity

List the different colours the class is wearing on the board. • How many men are wearing each
colour? • How many women are wearing each colour? • What is the class's favourite colour?

PAIRS OF CLOTHING

1. boots	8. old	15. shoes
2. boxer shorts	9. pair	16. shorts
3. gloves	10. pajamas	17. slippers
4. jeans	11. panties	18. sneakers
5. jockey shorts	12. pants (slacks)	19. socks
6. mittens	13. pantyhose	20. stockings
7. new	14. sandals	21. sunglasses

Group Game: *"True or false?"*

Work in groups of four. • Write three true statements about your clothes. • Write one false statement. • Read your statements to your group. • Who can guess the false statement?

Group Game: *"What am I wearing?"*

Describe one student's clothing from outside your group. • Who can guess that student's name?

WHAT ARE THEY WEARING?

With Your Class

Make a list on the board of the woman's clothing. Then make a list of the man's clothing.

She's wearing

_____

_____

_____

He's wearing

_____

_____

_____

_____

WHAT COLOUR ARE YOUR CLOTHES?

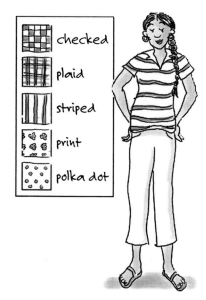

checked

plaid

striped

print

polka dot

This woman is wearing a grey and white striped T-shirt, white pants, and grey sandals. What colour are your clothes today?

Circle Dialogue

Do a circle dialogue with the question: "What colour are your clothes today?"

Teacher: "What colour are your clothes today?"

Student 1: "My shoes are _____,
(colour)

my pants are _____,
(colour)

my shirt is _____.
(colour)

What colour are your clothes today?"

Student 2:

_____

Continue around the circle.

11

FAMILY TREE

FAMILIES

Male	Female	Both Sexes
husband	wife	spouse
father	mother	parent
brother	sister	sibling*
son	daughter	child
grandson	granddaughter	grandchild
uncle	aunt	—
nephew	niece	—
—	—	cousin
		divorced person
		—
widower	widow	
father-in-law	mother-in-law	in-law
son-in-law	daughter-in-law	—
brother-in-law	sister-in-law	—
man (men)	woman (women)	adult
boy	girl	child (children)
		baby (babies)
		adolescent
		teenager
		youth
		young person
		(young people)

* *Siblings: brother, sister*

Questions

1. Which people in the picture are grandparents?
2. Which people are parents?
3. Which people are children?
4. How many uncles are there in the picture? How many aunts?
5. How many parents are there?
6. Who are in-laws?
7. Are the children cousins?
8. Which people are daughters? sons? brothers? siblings?
9. Which people are men? boys? women? girls?
10. How many **generations** do you see?

Group Discussion: Families

Choose a note taker for your group to take notes on your discussion and read the notes to the whole class afterwards.

1. Immediate families include only a father, mother, and children. How many immediate families are in the extended family picture?
2. Do people in your native country usually live together in immediate or extended family units?
3. If an extended family lives together, who is usually included? Who is the head of the household?
4. Do you prefer to live in an immediate or an extended family group? Why?
5. How many children do families usually have in your native country? What is considered a large family?
6. Who in your group comes from the largest immediate family? the smallest?
7. In the extended family picture, do you know the vocabulary for all the relationships? Where is the great-grandfather? the stepmother? the twins? the ex-husband? the great aunt? the second cousin? Identify all the relationships.
8. Does anyone in your group still have a great-grandparent living? How old is he or she?
9. Do any students in your group have twins in their family? triplets? quadruplets? quintuplets?

Partners' Activity: Your Family Tree

Draw your own family tree. Explain it to your partner. Then ask your partner these questions.

1. Are you married? What is your wife's (husband's) name?
2. Do you have any children? How many? How old are they? What are their names?
3. How many brothers and sisters do you have? How old are they? Where do they live? Are they married?
4. Do you have any nephews and nieces? How many?
5. Are your parents living? Where do they live? Are your grandparents living? When did they pass away (die)?

Your Family Tree

Using the family tree in the book, construct your own family tree by putting the names of your family members under each person. Draw extra people if your family has more members. Put an X through the people you do not need for your family tree. OR, on a separate piece of paper, draw your own family tree.

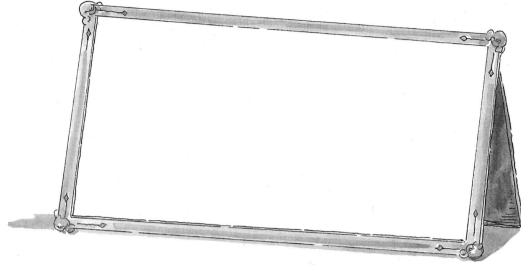

Tell the Class

Bring in photos of your family. • Show your photos to the class. • Explain who everyone is.

Tell the Class

Can you add more words to the list? • Tell the class about a favourite person in your family.

1. tall	5. thin	9. brown	13. bald	17. sympathetic
2. short	6. heavy	10. black	14. beard	18. funny
3. old	7. medium	11. grey	15. moustache	19. wise
4. young	8. blonde	12. red	16. helpful	

Partner Interview

Partner's name _____

Practise these questions with your teacher. • Then ask your partner.

1. Is your family big or small?
2. How many people are in your family?
3. How many brothers and sisters do you have?
4. Are they older or younger?
5. Do you have children?
6. Do you have a pet?

Draw

Work in groups of four or five. • Draw a family portrait or a family tree. • Tell your group about your family.

REVIEW

Partner Interview

Partner's name _____

Ask your partner.

1. What is your name?
2. What colour are your eyes?
3. What colour is your hair?
4. Are you tall or short?
5. Do you wear glasses?
6. Are you married?
7. How many sisters do you have?

8. How many brothers do you have?
9. How old are they?
10. What do they do?
11. Where do they live?
12. Where are you from?
13. What language do you speak?
14. What do you do?*

* *What do you/they do? means what work do you or they do?*

Find Someone Who

Review the vocabulary with your teacher. • *Fill in the name of someone who . . .*

1. _____ speaks three languages.
2. _____ has three names.
3. _____ is from a small family.
4. _____ is wearing jeans.
5. _____ is from a big city.
6. _____ wants to visit Canada's Wonderland.

UNIT 2

Everyday Life

THE CLASSROOM

1. board	8. desk	15. pen
2. book	9. door	16. pencil
3. ceiling	10. eraser	17. student
4. chair	11. floor	18. table
5. chalk	12. map	19. teacher
6. classroom	13. notebook	20. wall
7. clock	14. paper	21. window

Draw

Draw a picture of your classroom.• Include everything. • Work fast! • Compare pictures with the class. • Who had the most complete picture ?

Group Game: *"What is it?" or "Twenty questions"*

Work in groups of six. • Choose a leader.

Leader: *Think about something in the classroom. Don't say it!*

Class: *Ask the leader YES/NO questions.*

Leader: *Answer "Yes" or "No."*

Class: *Try to guess what it is. Whoever guesses is the new leader.*

TAKING A BREAK

1. arguing	7. going out	13. sitting	19. thinking
2. coming in	8. laughing	14. sleeping	20. walking
3. crying	9. listening	15. smiling	21. waving
4. drawing	10. looking	16. speaking	22. worrying
5 erasing	11. reading	17. standing	23. writing
6. frowning	12. shaking hands	18. talking	24. yawning

Think. • Write an activity. • Fold your paper. • Make a pile of papers. • Open one. • Follow the instruction. • Ask "What am I doing?" • Have the class guess the activity.

Partner Game: *"How are you today?"*   **Partner's name** _____

Decide how the people in the drawing are today. • Write in the bubbles. • Fill in your own.

1. angry	4. hot	7. sick
2. cold	5. hungry	8. tired
3. happy	6. nervous	9. thirsty

Group Vocabulary Challenge

Work in groups of four. • What do you do on a break? • Make a list with your group. • Read your group's list to the class. • With the class, make a list of the new words on the board. • Copy the new words into your notebook.

TIME

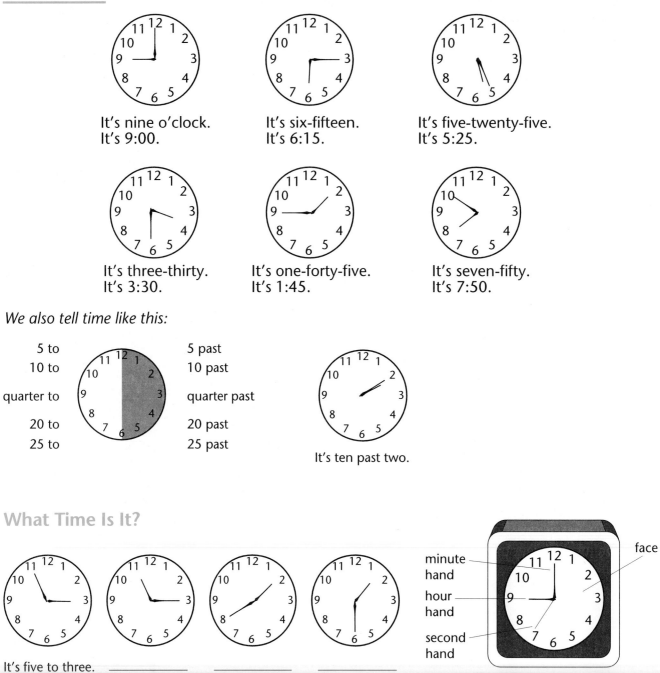

It's nine o'clock.
It's 9:00.

It's six-fifteen.
It's 6:15.

It's five-twenty-five.
It's 5:25.

It's three-thirty.
It's 3:30.

It's one-forty-five.
It's 1:45.

It's seven-fifty.
It's 7:50.

We also tell time like this:

5 to
10 to
quarter to
20 to
25 to

5 past
10 past
quarter past
20 past
25 past

It's ten past two.

What Time Is It?

It's five to three. _____ _____ _____

face
minute hand
hour hand
second hand

Questions for Conversation

Practise asking and answering these questions with your teacher. Then ask your partner the questions.

1. Are you wearing a watch?
2. Does it have a second hand?
3. What time is it?
4. Does this room have a clock?
5. Does it tell the same time as your watch?
6. What kind of clocks do you have at home?

_____   _____   _____

_____   _____

1. a.m.	7. night	13. alarm clock	19. eating lunch
2. p.m.	8. midnight	14. (wrist) watch	20. studying
3. morning	9. early	15. digital clock	21. eating dinner
4. noon	10. on time	16. waking up	22. going to bed
5. afternoon	11. late	17. eating breakfast	23. sleeping
6. evening	12. clock radio	18. going to class	

Class Discussion

What time is it in the pictures? • *What is the student doing?* • *Tell the picture story with your class.*

_____   _____

_____

Partner Interview

Partner's name _____

Practise these questions with your teacher. • Then ask your partner.

1. What time do you get up in the morning?
2. What time do you eat breakfast?
3. What time do you eat lunch?
4. What time do you eat dinner?
5. How many hours is your English class? What time does it start? What time does it end?
6. How many hours do you sleep at night?

Group Survey

Ask everyone in your group these questions. • Check YES or NO. • Count the answers . • Report your group's results to the class. • Write the class results on the board.

Do you:	YES	NO
1. get up early in the morning?	_____	_____
2. get up before 7:00 a.m.?	_____	_____
3. go to bed late at night?	_____	_____
4. go to bed after midnight? [1]	_____	_____
5. have an alarm clock?	_____	_____
6. come to class on time every day?	_____	_____
7. have lunch at noon? [2]	_____	_____

(1) Twelve o'clock at night (midnight)
(2) Twelve o'clock in the afternoon (noon)

EVERYDAY LIFE

A Mother's Day

A Worker's Day

1. does homework	6. goes to school	11. sweeps the floor
2. does laundry	7. goes to work	12. takes a break
3. feeds the baby	8. makes dinner	13. washes the dishes
4. gets a paycheque	9. punches in	14. works
5. goes shopping	10. reads to the children	

Class Discussion

Decide the correct time for each activity. • *Fill in the clocks.* • *Compare the everyday life of the mother and the worker.*

MORNING ROUTINE

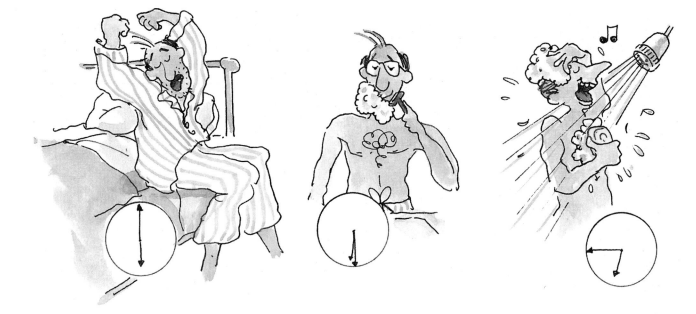

1. brush (his) teeth	5. get out of bed	9. say goodbye
2. comb (his) hair	6. leave for work	10. shave
3. drink coffee	7. make the bed	11. take a shower
4. get dressed	8. read the newspaper	12. watch the news

What's the Story?

Work in groups of three. • *Write a story about the man.* • *Everyone in the group should contribute three sentences.* • *Read your story to the class.*

Group Game: *"What do you do in the morning?"*

Work in groups of five. • *Pantomime one of these activities for your group.* • *No speaking!* • *Whoever guesses takes the next turn.*

Get out of bed.
Make the bed.
Take a shower.
Shave.
Comb your hair.
Brush your teeth.
Read the newspaper.
Watch TV
Drink coffee.
Leave for school.

REVIEW

Group Vocabulary Challenge

Work in groups of five. • *Make a list of all the vocabulary from your classroom.* • *Compare your list with another group.* • *Which group had the most new words?* • *Make a list of the new words on the board.* • *Copy the new words into your notebook.*

Class Activity

List ten questions about your day. • *Write them on the board.*

Partner Activity   Partner's name _____

Ask your partner the questions from the Class Activity. • *Present your interview to the class.*

Partner Game: *"What do you do every day?"*   Partner's name_____

Take turns. • *Pantomime what you do every day.* • *No speaking!* • *Let your partner guess.* • *List five of the activities.* • *Show your class what your partner does every day.*

UNIT 3

The Calendar

DAYS OF THE WEEK

	SUNDAY	MONDAY	TUESDAY	WEDNESDAY	THURSDAY	FRIDAY	SATURDAY
MORNING							
AFTERNOON							
EVENING							

1. Sunday	8. today	15. weekday
2. Monday	9. yesterday	16. weekend
3. Tuesday	10. tomorrow	17. ago
4. Wednesday	11. the day before yesterday	18. last
5. Thursday	12. the day after tomorrow	19. next
6. Friday	13. calendar	
7. Saturday	14. week	

Write

What are you doing every day this week? • *Fill in the calendar.* • *Explain it to your partner.*

Practise these questions with your teacher. • *Then ask your partner.*

1. What day is today?
2. What day is tomorrow?
3. What day was yesterday? What did you do yesterday?
4. What day was the day before yesterday?
5. What are you going to do next weekend?
6. What did you do last weekend?
7. Did you come to class last week?
8. Which is your favourite day? Why?
9. What are the days of the week?
10. How many days are there in a weekend? Name them.

Group Survey

Ask everyone in your group these questions. • *Check YES, NO, or SOMETIMES.* • *Count the answers.* • *Report your group's results to the class.* • *Write the class' results on the board.*

Do you:	YES	NO	SOMETIMES
1. sleep late on Sundays?	_____	_____	_____
2. shop on Saturday afternoons?	_____	_____	_____
3. study late in the evening?	_____	_____	_____
4. go to the movies on Friday evenings?	_____	_____	_____
5. work on the weekends?	_____	_____	_____

MONTHS AND DATES

JANUARY	FEBRUARY	MARCH	APRIL
MAY	JUNE	JULY	AUGUST
SEPTEMBER	OCTOBER	NOVEMBER	DECEMBER

first (1st)	eleventh (11th)	twenty-first (21st)	month
second (2nd)	twelfth (12th)	twenty-second (22nd)	year
third (3rd)	thirteenth (13th)	twenty-third (23rd)	leap year
fourth (4th)	fourteenth (14th)	twenty-fourth (24th)	century
fifth (5th)	fifteenth (15th)	twenty-fifth (25th)	
sixth (6th)	sixteenth (16th)	twenty-sixth (26th)	
seventh (7th)	seventeenth (17th)	twenty-seventh (27th)	
eighth (8th)	eighteenth (18th)	twenty-eighth (28th)	
ninth (9th)	nineteenth (19th)	twenty-ninth (29th)	
tenth (10th)	twentieth (20th)	thirtieth (30th)	
		thirty-first (31st)	

Class Discussion

1. What is the date today?
2. What was last month?
3. What is next month?
4. What date does this course end?
5. What is the date of the next holiday?
6. When is the next leap year?
7. What century is this?
8. How many days in a week?
9. How many weeks are there in a year?
10. How many months are there in a year?
11. How many years are there in a century?
12. What is a decade?
13. How many days are there in each month?
14. What is a leap year? How many days are there in a leap year?
15. What is the year now?
16. What was last year?
17. What will next year be?

Group Activity

Work in groups of five or six. • Decide on important dates. • Write them on your calendars. • Compare your dates with the class.

Include:

1. your birthdays
2. other important dates
3. important holidays in your countries

Class Game: *"What is your favourite month?"*

Think. • Write. • Fold. • Make a pile. • Open one. • Read it to the class. • Guess who wrote it.

BIRTHDAYS

1. balloon	8. fork	15. party
2. blow out the candles	9. Happy Birthday!	16. party hat
3. cake	10. horn	17. present
4. candle	11. knife	18. punch
5. celebrate	12. make a wish	19. spoon
6. cup	13. napkin	20. surprise
7. decorations	14. paper plate	21. table

What's the Story?

Work in groups of four. • *Write a story about the birthday party.* • *Everyone in the group should contribute at least one sentence.* • *Read your story to the class.*

1. What kind of celebration is this?
2. Whose birthday do you think it is?
3. How old is s/he?
4. What is on the table?
5. What do you think the presents are?

Partner Interview

Partner's name _____

Practise these questions with your teacher. • *Then ask your partner.*

1. What do you like to give as a birthday gift? to a friend? to a parent? to a co-worker? to a teacher? to a child?
2. When is your birthday? (or your name day?)
3. What kind of birthday cake is your favourite?
4. Describe how you like to celebrate your birthday (or your name day).

Write

Partner's name_____

When is your partner's birthday? • *Write a message to your partner on the card.* • *Sign the birthday card.* • *Give it to your partner.* • *Read your message to your partner.*

Cross-Cultural Exchange

Do people celebrate birthdays in your country? • *Do they celebrate name days?* • *Tell the class how they celebrate.* • *How do you say "Happy Birthday" in your native language?* • *Teach the class.*

NATIONAL HOLIDAYS

Date: _____   Date: _____

Date: _____

Class Activity

Fill in the dates this year with your class.   •   What is your favourite holiday?   •   Tell the class.

Conversation Squares

Work in groups of three.   •   First write your own answers.   •   Then ask your partners the questions.   •   Write their answers.   •   Compare your group's answers with other groups.

Favourite	You _____	Partner 1_____	Partner 2_____
holiday	_____	_____	_____
holiday food	_____	_____	_____
holiday activity	_____	_____	_____

36

Date: _____

Date: _____

Date: _____

1. New Year's Eve
2. champagne
3. streamers
4. Happy New Year
5. midnight
6. party hats
7. Canada Day

8. flag
9. parade
10. Mounties
11. fireworks
12. band
13. long weekend
14. Thanksgiving

15. turkey
16. pumpkin pie
17. cranberry sauce
18. harvest
19. autumn
20. Christmas
21. tree

22. Christmas lights
23. Santa Claus
24. Merry Christmas!
25. reindeer
26. presents

CHRISTMAS IN CANADA

Matching

Match these pictures with the activities:

1. baking Christmas cookies and fruitcakes
2. Christmas pageants
3. decorating the tree
4. Christmas shopping
5. sending Christmas cards and gifts
6. opening Christmas gifts

Questions for Conversation

1. Do you celebrate Christmas?
2. Do you have a Christmas tree at Christmas? What do you decorate it with?
3. Do you give Christmas presents? To whom?
4. Do you eat any special food at Christmastime? What food?
5. In Canada, Christmas is both a religious holiday for Christians and a national holiday for everyone. In your native country, is there any holiday that is both a religious and a national holiday? Tell about it.
6. Christmas is the biggest holiday in Canada. What is the biggest holiday in your native country? How do people celebrate it?

SPECIAL DAYS

Date: _____

Date: _____

Date: _____

Date: _____

Date: _____

1. Valentine's Day	7. Mother	13. witch
2. chocolates	8. Father	14. costume
3. flowers	9. Halloween	15. Trick or Treat!
4. candy	10. jack-o'-lantern	16. Happy Halloween!
5. I love you!	11. pumpkin	17. soldiers
6. Happy Valentine's Day	12. ghost	18. cemetery

Conversation Activity

1. Do you celebrate these special days in your country?
2. What is your favourite holiday food?
3. How do you say "Merry Christmas" and "Happy New Year" in your native language?
4. What is your favourite holiday? Tell the class about it (What is the date? What special foods and activities are part of this holiday?)

SEASONS

1. beach	8. garden	14. rake	21. snowsuit
2. beach towel	9. harvest	15. sand	22. tulip
3. bird	10. ice	16. seedlings	23. volleyball
4. cider	11. leaf	17. shovel	24. water
5. cooler	12. nest	18. snow	25. waves
6. egg	13. plow	19. snowball	
7. farm stand		20. snowman	

Class Discussion

1. Where you live now, are the seasons the same as in the pictures?
2. What happens in each season?
3. What do you like to do in each season?
4. Which season is your favourite?
5. Are the seasons the same in your native city? What is different? What is the same?

What's the Story?

Work in groups of three. • Choose one season. • Write a story. • Everyone in the group should contribute at least two sentences. • Read your story to the class.

1. What are the people wearing?
2. What are they doing?
3. Do they like what they are doing?

Partner Game: *"What do you remember?"*   Partner's name _____

Look at the picture with your partner. • Remember as much as you can. • Close your book. • Describe the picture with your partner. • List everything.   • Compare your notes with another pair of students. • Add to your list.

WEATHER

1. bench	7. earmuffs	12. hill	18. rain	23. umbrella
2. branches	8. grass	13. leaves	19. rake	24. warm
3. clear	9. hail	14. lightning	20. shine	25. wet
4. cloud	10. hailstorm	15. muffler	21. splash	26. windy
5. cloudy	11. hat	16. picnic	22. thunder	
6. cool		17. puddle		

Class Discussion

What are the people doing in the pictures? • *What are they thinking?*

42

Partner Interview

Partner's name _____

Practise these questions with your teacher. • *Then ask your partner.*

What do you like to do:

1. on a rainy day?
2. on a sunny day?

3. on a cold day?
4. on a snowy day?

Find Someone Who

Review the vocabulary with your teacher. • *Fill in the name of someone who . . .*

1. _____ has never seen snow.
2. _____ has been in a hail storm.
3. _____ has been in a thunderstorm.
4. _____ likes rain.
5. _____ likes winter.
6. _____ likes to be outdoors in cold weather.
7. _____ likes to be outdoors in hot weather.
8. _____ has seen a tornado.

WEATHER REPORT

1. weather map	8. cloudy	14. south	21. Great Lakes
2. meteorologist	9. showers	15. freezing rain	22. Rockies
3. cool	10. thunderstorm	16. fog	23. West Coast
4. rainy	11. snowflakes	17. drizzle	24. East Coast
5. mild	12. temperature	18. clearing	25. Territory
6. dry	13. north	19. Maritimes	
7. sunny		20. Prairies	

SEASONAL CLOTHING

1. bathing suit	7. long underwear	13. shorts	19. sun hat
2. bikini	8. overcoat	14. ski jacket	20. swim trunks
3. boots	9. poncho	15. ski pants	21. tank top
4. cutoffs	10. rain hat	16. slicker	22. T-shirt
5. earmuffs	11. rubbers	17. snow suit	23. umbrella
6. halter	12. scarf	18. stocking cap	24. vest

Partner Interview

Partner's name _____

Practise these questions with your teacher. • *Then ask your partner.*

1. What do you wear in cold weather?
2. What do you wear when it rains?
3. What do you wear in hot weather?
4. What do you wear when you go to the beach?
5. What do you wear when you go on a picnic?

Speech

Tell the class about the weather in your hometown. • *Use these questions as a guide:*

1. Are there seasons in your hometown? What are they? When are they?
2. What is the weather like in each season?
3. What do people wear in each season?

REVIEW

Partner's name _____

Ask your partner.

1. What is today's date?
2. What's the weather like today?
3. Is it hot? cold? warm? cool?
4. What season is it?
5. Do you like this weather?
6. What do you want to do today?

Write

Write in your journal.

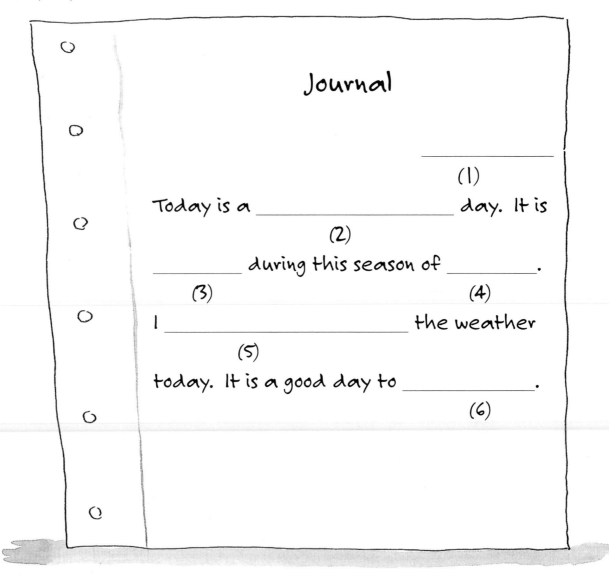

Tell Your Partner

Read your journal entry to your partner. • *Listen to your partner's journal.*

UNIT 4

NET. WT.
240 gms.

CARVER FOTINOS

FOOD

FRUIT

1. apple	7. cherry	13. lime	19. pineapple	25. core
2. apricot	8. coconut	14. mango	20. plum	26. pit
3. banana	9. grape	15. orange	21. raspberry	27. skin
4. blackberry	10. grapefruit	16. peach	22. strawberry	28. box
5. blueberry	11. kiwi	17. pear	23. watermelon	29. bunch
6. cantaloupe	12. lemon	18. papaya	24. seeds	30. kilo

Partner Interview   **Partner's name** _____

Practise these questions with your teacher. • *Then ask your partner.*

1. What is your favourite fruit?
2. What other fruits do you like?
3. What fruits grow in your country?
4. What fruits can you buy in your neighbourhood?
5. Are there fruits that grow in your country that you don't find in Canada?
6. What *new* fruits do you find in Canada?

Group Game: *"Preparing fruit salad"*

Work in groups of four. • *Prepare a fruit salad for the next class.*

To Get Ready:
What fruit will each student bring?

_____   _____

_____   _____

Important Verbs

cut	slice	wash	scoop	pit
peel	chop	rinse	core	mix

Who will bring a bowl?   _____

Who will bring a knife?   _____

Who will bring a large spoon?   _____

Who will bring a fork?   _____

To Demonstrate:
• *Prepare your fruit salad.*

• *Compare the fruit salads.*

• *Vote on the best one.*

• *Enjoy the snack!*

49

VEGETABLES

1. artichoke	7. cabbage	15. eggplant	23. peas	30. squash
2. asparagus	8. carrots	16. green pepper	24. peeled	31. stalk
3. beans	9. cauliflower	17. head	25. pepper	32. turnip
4. beets	10. celery	18. kilo	26. potato	33. yams
5. broccoli	11. cooked	19. lettuce	27. radish	34. zucchini
6. bunch	12. corn	20. mushrooms	28. raw	
	13. cucumber	21. onions	29. spinach	
	14. ear	22. parsnip		

Partner Interview

Practise these questions with your teacher. • *Then ask your partner.*

1. What is your favourite vegetable? _____
2. What vegetables don't you like?
3. What vegetables grow in your country?
4. Which vegetables do you usually use for salad?
5. What do these vegetables usually cost at your market?
6. Which vegetables do you buy by the bunch? by the head? by the ear? by the kilo?

_____

Group Decision

Work in groups of five or six. • *Decide which vegetables to use for a salad.* • *Decide how to prepare each vegetable.* • *Tell the class about your salad.*

VEGETABLE	YES/NO	COOKED	RAW	PEELED	SLICED	SHREDDED	CHOPPED
	___	___	___	___	___	___	___
	___	___	___	___	___	___	___
	___	___	___	___	___	___	___
	___	___	___	___	___	___	___
	___	___	___	___	___	___	___
	___	___	___	___	___	___	___
	___	___	___	___	___	___	___
	___	___	___	___	___	___	___
other	___	___	___	___	___	___	___
	___	___	___	___	___	___	___

MEAT, SEAFOOD, AND POULTRY

1. can	7. lamb roast	13. package	19. shrimp
2. chicken	8. leg of lamb	14. pig's feet	20. steak
3. ground beef	9. liver	15. pork chops	21. stew beef
4. ham	10. lobster	16. roast beef	22. swordfish
5. hot dogs	11. meatballs	17. salmon	23. tuna fish
6. lamb chops	12. octopus	18. sausages	24. turkey

Partner Interview   Partner's name _____

Practise these questions with your teacher. • Then ask your partner.

1. Do you eat meat? What is your favourite meat?
2. Do you eat poultry? What is your favourite?
3. Do you eat seafood? What is your favourite fish? What is your favourite shellfish?
4. Which meats, fish, and poultry are most common in your country?
5. Are there any meats, fish, or poultry that you never eat? Why?
6. Where do you buy meats? fish? poultry?
7. Is it a good idea to eat a lot of red meat? Why? Why not? Is it healthy?

PREPARING MEAT, FISH, AND SEAFOOD

1. bake	4. broil	7. grill	10. seasoning
2. barbecue	5. casserole	8. microwave	11. simmer
3. boil	6. fry	9. roast	12. stir fry

Find Someone Who

How do you like your food prepared? • *Review the vocabulary with your teacher.* • *Fill in the name of someone who . . .*

1. _____ likes baked fish with salt and pepper.
2. _____ prepares barbecued spare ribs.
3. _____ doesn't eat fried food.
4. _____ knows how to prepare stir fry.
5. _____ likes meat simmered in sauce.
6. _____ likes casseroles.
7. _____ likes food with chili powder.
8. _____ broils steak with seasoning.
9. _____ is a vegetarian.

DESSERTS

1. beverage	6. cheesecake	11. doughnut	16. ice cream soda	21. pastry
2. brownie	7. coffee	12. espresso	17. iced coffee	22. pie
3. cake	8. coffee cake	13. frozen yogurt	18. iced tea	23. pie a la mode
4. candy	9. cone	14. glass of water	19. lemonade	24. sherbet
5. cappuccino	10. cookies	15. ice cream	20. milk shake	25. sundae

What's the Story?

Work in groups of five. • Choose one table. • Write a story about the people. • Everyone in the group should contribute at least two sentences. • Read your story to the class.

1. Who are the people?
2. Where are they?
3. What are they eating?
4. What are the children's favourite desserts?
5. What are the adults' favourite desserts?

Group Discussion

Work in groups of five. • *Discuss these questions.* • *Report your answers to the class.*

1. What is your favourite dessert?
2. Do you buy it or prepare it?
3. How do you prepare it?
4. Is it fattening?
5. How often do you have your favourite dessert?

INTERNATIONAL DESSERT MENU

Group Role Play

Work in groups of five. • *First, fill in this menu with the desserts your group likes.* • *Decide on prices.* • *Then write a role play ordering dessert and coffee (or tea) at a coffee shop.* • *Present your role play to the class.*

Cross-Cultural Exchange

Bring your favourite desserts or pastries to class • *Take a break.* • *Have a dessert party.* • *Taste everyone's dessert!* • *Write the recipe.* • *Exchange recipes with your classmates.*

BREAKFAST

1. bacon	7. cream	13. jelly	19. orange juice
2. bagel	8. cream cheese	14. jam	20. pancakes
3. butter	9. danish	15. margarine	21. rice
4. cereal	10. French toast	16. milk	22. sugar
5. cereal bowl	11. (fried) egg	17. muffin	23. syrup
6. cocoa	12. home fries	18. oatmeal	24. toast

Partner Interview

Partner's name _____

Practise these questions with your teacher. • *Then ask your partner.*

1. What is a typical breakfast for you?
2. What time do you eat breakfast?
3. Do you eat breakfast with your family?
4. Do you eat breakfast at home?
5. In your opinion, what is a healthy breakfast?

Cross-Cultural Exchange

What do people usually eat for breakfast in your country? • *Tell the class.* • *Add new vocabulary to the list.*

Conversation Squares

Work in groups of three. • *First write your own answers.* • *Then ask your partners the questions.* • *Write their answers.* • *Compare your group's answers with other groups.*

Breakfast	You _____	Partner 1_____	Partner 2_____
today	_____	_____	_____
yesterday	_____	_____	_____
tomorrow	_____	_____	_____

Group Survey

Ask everyone in your group these questions. • *Check ALWAYS, SOMETIMES, or NEVER.* • *Count the answers.* • *Report your group's results to the class.* • *Write the class's results on the board.*

How often do you:	ALWAYS	SOMETIMES	NEVER
1. skip breakfast?	_____	_____	_____
2. drink coffee for breakfast?	_____	_____	_____
3. have cold cereal for breakfast?	_____	_____	_____
4. have hot cereal for breakfast?	_____	_____	_____
5. have fruit or fruit juice for breakfast?	_____	_____	_____
6. have something sweet for breakfast?	_____	_____	_____
7. eat out for breakfast?	_____	_____	_____
8. eat a nutritious breakfast?	_____	_____	_____

LUNCH

1. bread	12. hot dog	23. potato chips
2. brown paper bag	13. ketchup	24. rice
3. bologna	14. leftovers	25. roast beef
4. cafeteria	15. lunchbox	26. salad
5. cheese	16. lunchroom	27. salami
6. coffee mug	17. mayonnaise	28. sandwich
7. cold cuts	18. microwave oven	29. soup
8. french fries	19. mustard	30. spaghetti
9. frozen entree	20. peanut butter	31. spaghetti sauce
10. ham	21. pizza	32. thermos
11. hero (submarine)	22. plastic baggie	33. yogurt

What's the Story?

Work in groups of five. • *Choose one scene from the illustration above and write a story.* • *Everyone in the group should contribute at least two sentences.* • *Read your story to the class.*

1. Where are the people?
2. What are their names?
3. What are they eating and drinking?
4. What are they saying?

Partner Interview

Practise these questions with your teacher. • *Then ask your partner.*

1. What time do you usually eat lunch?
2. Where do you eat lunch?
3. What do you usually eat for lunch?
4. What do you usually drink for lunch?
5. Do you usually eat a nutritious lunch?
6. Do you ever skip lunch? Why?
7. Do you bring your lunch to work? (to school?) What do you bring?
8. Do you make your own lunch? If not, who makes it for you?
9. If you buy your lunch, where do you buy it? How much does it cost?
10. Who do you usually eat lunch with? What do you talk about?

Write

What is your favourite sandwich? • *How do you prepare it?* • *Write the recipe.* • *Tell the class how to make your favourite sandwich.*

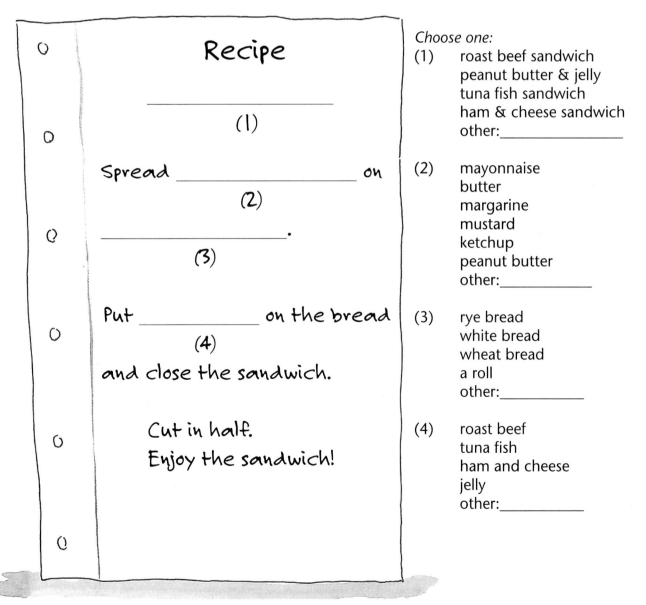

Recipe

_____
(1)

Spread _____ on
(2)

_____ .
(3)

Put _____ on the bread
(4)

and close the sandwich.

Cut in half.
Enjoy the sandwich!

Choose one:
(1) roast beef sandwich
     peanut butter & jelly
     tuna fish sandwich
     ham & cheese sandwich
     other:_____

(2) mayonnaise
     butter
     margarine
     mustard
     ketchup
     peanut butter
     other:_____

(3) rye bread
     white bread
     wheat bread
     a roll
     other:_____

(4) roast beef
     tuna fish
     ham and cheese
     jelly
     other:_____

FAST FOOD

1. bun	8. fries	15. onion rings	22. soda (pop)
2. chicken nuggets	9. hamburger	16. order	23. straw
3. coffee	10. hot sauce (salsa)	17. pickle	24. tacos
4. counter	11. large	18. pizza	25. tea
5. customer	12. line	19. salad bar	
6. drive-in window	13. medium	20. shake	
7. fried chicken	14. milk	21. small	

Can you name some "fast food" restaurants in your city? Do you like to eat in a fast food restaurant? When? Why?

Group Survey

Ask everyone in your group these questions. • Check YES or NO. • Count the answers. • Report your group's results to the class. • Write the class' results on the board.

Do you:	YES	NO
1. ever eat fast food?	_____	_____
2. like hamburgers with "the works"?	_____	_____
3. like french fries?	_____	_____
4. like ketchup on your fries?	_____	_____
5. like pizza?	_____	_____
6. like hot dogs?	_____	_____
7. like mustard on your hot dogs?	_____	_____
8. like tacos?	_____	_____
9. like hot salsa?	_____	_____
10. think fast food is bad for you?	_____	_____

Partner Role Play

With your partner, complete this role play. • Present your role play to the class.

Cashier: May I help you?
Customer: _____

Cashier: Anything to drink?
Customer: _____

Cashier: Anything else?
Customer: _____

Cashier: That'll be $ _____.__ please.

(Customer gives cashier $20.00. Cashier takes change out of the cash register and gives back change.)

Cashier: That's $_____ change. Have a nice day.

JUNK FOOD

1. bubble gum	5. corn chips	9. peanuts	13. tortilla chips
2. candy bar	6. crackers	10. popcorn	14. vending machine
3. cheese snack	7. gum	11. pretzels	
4. chocolate bar	8. juice drink	12. soda	

Class Discussion

1. Which junk foods do you like? Which don't you like?
2. Do you ever eat junk food? When?
3. Where do you buy junk food?

Class Game: *"What is your favourite junk food?"*

Write the name of your favourite junk food. • Fold your paper. • Make a pile. • Open one. • Guess who wrote the paper. • Who likes the same junk food?

Group Decision

Work in groups of five or six. • Your group has $5.00 to spend on snacks. • Look at the illustration. • What will you buy from the machines? • Tell the class.

DINNER

1. beer	6. hostess	11. smoking section
2. busboy	7. maitre d'	12. tip
3. cashier	8. no smoking section	13. waiter
4. cheque	9. restaurant	14. waitress
5. drink	10. rest room	15. wine

What's the Story?

Work in groups of five. • Choose one table and write a story. • Everyone in the group should contribute at least one sentence. • Read your story to the class.

1. Who are the people? What are their names?
2. Why have they gone out to eat tonight?
3. What are they having for dinner?
4. How are they feeling tonight?
5. What are they saying?
6. Who will pay the cheque?
7. What will they do after they leave the restaurant?

THE SUPERMARKET

Practise this Vocabulary

1. aisle	7. beverages	13. condiments	19. paper products
2. baby products	8. coffee and tea	14. express line	20. produce
3. bakery	9. check-out counter	15. frozen foods	21. shopping cart
4. cash register	10. courtesy desk	16. groceries	22. snack foods and candy
5. cashier	11. dairy section	17. line up	
6. canned goods	12. deli counter	18. meat section	

Class Discussion

1. Do you buy food in a supermarket? Which one?
2. Are the prices expensive or reasonable?
3. Do you ever buy anything at the deli (delicatessen) counter? What do you buy?
4. What dairy products do you buy?
5. What other sections are there in your supermarket?
6. Do you ever cash cheques in the supermarket? Do you have a cheque-cashing card? Do you ever use a debit card?
7. Are there supermarkets in your native country (or city)? Do they give plastic or paper bags to shoppers for groceries? What differences are there between a supermarket in your native country (or city) and a supermarket in Canada?
8. When is your supermarket busiest? Why? When do you like to shop? Why?
9. What do you usually buy in the supermarket?

COMPARING PRICES

Comparison Shopping at the Supermarket

The small jar has half as much applesauce as the large one. Both jars are 99¢. Which one is cheaper?

Which one is the better buy?

Which can of peas is smaller?

Which can is cheaper?

Which can of peas is a better buy?

Class Discussion

*Some brands are famous. They are sold in many different stores. They are called **name brands**. Other brands are made especially for one supermarket chain. They are called **store brands**. Store brands are usually cheaper than name brands. • Discuss with your class the name brands and store brands you know for each of these items. Are the name brands better than the store brands?*

1. bread   2. ketchup   3. cheese   4. juices   5. Other:...

Class Discussion: Saving Money at the Supermarket

What are some ways you can save money at the supermarket? Talk about the pictures. Add your own idea.

COMPARISON SHOPPING

Questions for Conversation

1. Where can you buy combs and brushes?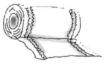

2. Where can you buy paper plates and cups? When do you use them?

3. Where can you buy paper towels? What can you use them for?

4. Where can you buy disposable diapers? How do you dispose of them when they are dirty?

5. Where can you buy deodorant? What brands do you know of?

6. What kinds of medicine can you buy in a supermarket?

7. What kind of tissues do you usually buy?

8. What kind of soap do you usually buy?

9. What kind of toothpaste do you usually buy?

10. What kind of shampoo do you usually buy?

Community Activity

Is it cheaper to buy these items in one store than another? Compare the prices of the items on this page at two different stores in your community. Report to the class.

REVIEW

Group Decision

*Work in groups of five or six. • Choose one
of the family pictures. • Plan menus for
one day (breakfast, lunch, dinner and
snacks) for the family. • Figure the cost.*

Breakfast

$_____

Lunch

$_____

Dinner

$_____

Snacks

$_____

Class Game: *"What is it?"*

Choose a leader.

> **Leader:** *Think of a food you like. Don't say it!*
> **Class:** *Ask the leader YES/NO questions.*
> **Leader:** *Answer "Yes" or "No."*
> **Class:** *Try to guess the food. Whoever guesses is the new leader.*

Cross-Cultural Exchange

*Bring special foods from your country to class. • Have an international party. • Bring tapes of
music from your country to play at the party. • Enjoy!*

UNIT 5

HOMES

CITY OR COUNTRY

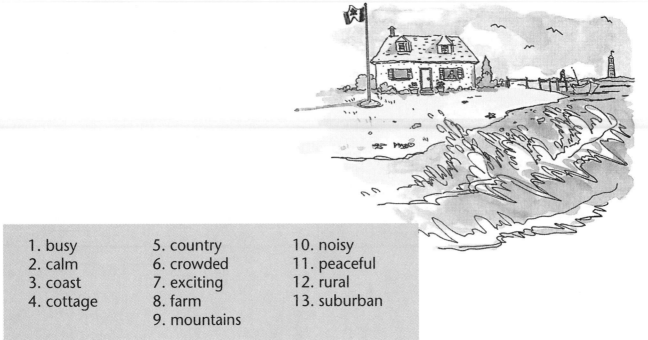

1. busy	5. country	10. noisy
2. calm	6. crowded	11. peaceful
3. coast	7. exciting	12. rural
4. cottage	8. farm	13. suburban
	9. mountains	

Interview Questions

Practise asking and answering these questions with your teacher. Then ask your partner the questions. Finally, present your interview to the class.

1. Where do you live now? Is it a city? Is it a town? Is it in the mountains? Is it in the country?
2. What street do you live on? What is your address?
3. Where were you born? In the city or in the country?
4. Which do you prefer—the city or the country? Why?
5. Which do you prefer—the mountains, the country, or the beach? Why?

HOMES

1. apartment (flat)	7. cement	13. garage	19. porch
2. attic	8. chimney	14. garden	20. roof
3. balcony	9. condominium	15. home	21. terrace
4. basement	10. dormitory	16. house	22. wood
5. brick	11. fence	17. mobile home	23. yard
6. bungalow	12. floor	18. motel	

What's the Story?

Work in groups of three. • Decide which home to describe. • Write a story about the home and the people. • Everyone in the group should contribute at least two sentences. • Read your story to the class.

Conversation Squares

Work in groups of four. • First write your own answers. • Then ask your partners the questions. • Write their answers. • Compare your group's answers with the other groups. • Make a class directory.

1. What's your name? First/Middle/Last: _____ **What's your address?** Number/Street _____ Apartment Number _____ City or Town _____ Province _____ Postal Code _____ **What's your phone number?** Area Code: (_____) Number: _____	**3. What's your name?** First/Middle/Last: _____ **What's your address?** Number/Street _____ Apartment Number _____ City or Town _____ Province _____ Postal Code _____ **What's your phone number?** Area Code: (_____) Number: _____
2. What's your name? First/Middle/Last: _____ **What's your address?** Number/Street _____ Apartment Number _____ City or Town _____ Province _____ Postal Code _____ **What's your phone number?** Area Code: (_____) Number: _____	**4. What's your name?** First/Middle/Last: _____ **What's your address?** Number/Street _____ Apartment Number _____ City or Town _____ Province _____ Postal Code _____ **What's your phone number?** Area Code: (_____) Number: _____

THE KITCHEN

1. Where is the family?
2. What are their names?
3. What time is it?
4. What is the family doing?

1. burner	8. dryer	15. microwave oven	22. tea kettle
2. cabinet	9. electric can opener	16. oven	23. toaster
3. coffee maker	10. electric mixer	17. pot	24. washing machine
4. creamer	11. faucet	18. refrigerator	25. wok
5. cupboard	12. freezer	19. sink	
6. dishpan	13. frying pan	20. stove	
7. dishwasher	14. linoleum	21. sugar bowl	

One partner looks at the picture on this page. • The other partner looks at the picture on page 74. • Compare kitchens. • List everything in both kitchens. • What is the same? • What is different? • What do you have in your kitchen? • Compare the kitchen in your country to your Canadian kitchen.

THE DINING ROOM

1. buffet	8. mirror	15. salt shaker	22. table
2. candlestick	9. napkin	16. saucer	23. tablecloth
3. chair	10. pepper shaker	17. serving spoon	24. tablespoon
4. cup	11. pie server	18. set the table	25. teaspoon
5. fork	12. pitcher	19. silverware	26. vase
6. glass	13. plate	20. soup bowl	
7. knife	14. salad bowl	21. spoon	

Practise these questions with your teacher. • Then ask your partner.
1. What room do you eat in at home?
2. How do you set the table at home? for breakfast? lunch? dinner?
3. Does your family always eat together?

Group Activity

Work in groups of four or five. • With your group, list five things people say at the dinner table. • Read your list to the class. • Make a list on the board.

Group Role Play

Work in groups of five. • Choose one scene. • Write a role play with your group. • Include roles for everyone. • Present your role play to the class.
1. a family eating together
2. a family setting the table for dinner with guests
3. a teenager eating with his (or her) friends in the kitchen

Include in your role play:
1. the people (give them names!)   4. what is on the table
2. how they feel   5. the food
3. what they are saying

Cross-Cultural Exchange

What are some traditional eating customs in your country? • Tell the class. • How are the customs the same in different countries? • Which countries are the most similar?

THE LIVING ROOM

1. armchair	7. fireplace	14. picture	21. stereo
2. bookcase	8. lamp	15. plant	22. television (TV)
3. carpet	9. lampshade	16. radio	23. throw pillow
4. CD player	10. laser disc player	17. relax	24. VCR
5. coffee table	11. listen to music	18. rug	25. watch TV
6. drapes	12. nap	19. sofa (couch)	
	13. photograph	20. speakers	

Group Vocabulary Challenge

Work in groups of four. • Make a list of everything you do in your living rooms. • Read your list to the class. • Which group had the most new words? • Make a list on the board. • Copy the new words into your notebook.

Class Game: *"What do you do in the living room?"*

Think. • Write an activity. • Fold your paper. • Make a pile of papers. • Open one. • Follow the instruction. • Ask "What am I doing?" • Have the class guess the activity.

Group Game: *"Gossip!"*

Work in groups of eight. • Choose a leader. • Close your books. • Look at the cover. • What are the people saying?

Leader: *(To the first student) Read the secret on page 226. Close your book. Whisper the secret to the student sitting next to you.*

Next Student: *Whisper the secret to the student sitting next to you, etc.*

Last Student: *Write the secret on the board or tell the class.*

Class: *Check the secret on page 226. Which group had the most accurate secret?*

Community Activity

Bring in flyers from stores that sell furniture. • Decide as a class how to furnish a living room. • What will you buy? • How much will each item cost? • What will the total bill be?

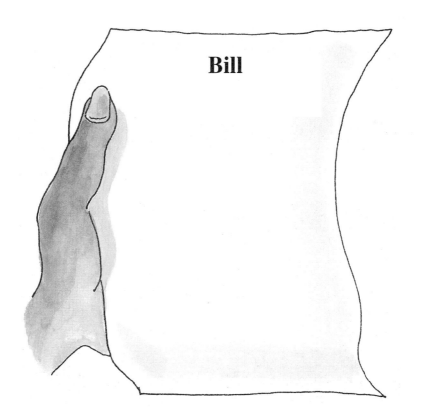

Bill

THE BEDROOM

What are the people doing?

Do bedrooms in your native country look the same or different than the one in this picture? Please explain.

1. bedspread	6. chest	11. dresser	16. night table
2. blanket	7. clock	12. head board	17. pillowcase
3. box spring	8. closet	13. lamp	18. shade
4. brush	9. curtains	14. mattress	19. sheets
5. carpet	10. drawer	15. mirror	20. telephone

Look at the picture. • Remember as much as you can. • Close your book. • List everything. • Compare your answers with the class. • Who had the longest list? • Open your book and check your answers.

Fill in the blanks and read the sentences with your class.

1. When you make a bed, you put on a _____, two _____, and a _____ . You put a _____ on the pillow.

2. On this window, there is a _____ and _____ . At night, you pull down the _____ .

3. You hang your clothes in the _____ . You fold other clothes and put them in the _____ or the _____ .

4. At night, you climb into _____, cover up with the _____ and _____, switch off the _____, lay your head on the _____, and go to sleep. Sweet dreams!

Draw

Draw a picture of your childhood bedroom. • Explain your picture to your partner.

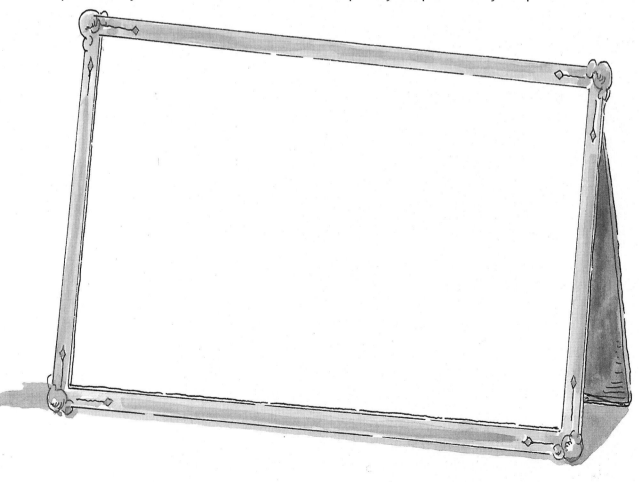

THE BATHROOM

1. aspirin	8. conditioner	15. shampoo	22. toilet
2. band aid	9. deodorant	16. shaving cream	23. toilet paper
3. bath mat	10. drain	17. shower curtain	24. toilet seat
4. bath towel	11. electric razor	18. soap	25. toothbrush
5. bath toy	12. medicine cabinet	19. soap dish	26. toothpaste
6. bathtub	13. mirror	20. tap (faucet)	27. towel
7. bubble bath	14. razor	21. tiles	

What's the Story?

Work in groups of three. • Write a story about the bathroom. • Everyone in the group should contribute at least three sentences. • Read your story to the class.

1. What time of day is it?
2. Who are the people?
3. What are their names?

4. What are they doing?
5. What are they going to do?
6. What are they thinking?

Cross-Cultural Exchange

Are baths or showers more popular in your country? • Is the toilet in the same room as the bath? • Do children use training toilets? • Do people sing in the shower or bath?

AT HOME

Class Vocabulary Challenge

Make a list of the vocabulary words you can remember. • Read your list to the class. • Who has the most new words? • Make a list on the board. • Copy the new words into your notebook.

Group Survey

Ask everyone in your group these questions. • Check ALWAYS, SOMETIMES, or NEVER. • Count the answers. • Report your group's results to the class. • Write the class's results on the board.

How often do you:	ALWAYS	SOMETIMES	NEVER
1. eat lunch at home?	_____	_____	_____
2. watch TV in the evening?	_____	_____	_____
3. read magazines in the bathtub?	_____	_____	_____
4. write letters in the kitchen?	_____	_____	_____
5. talk on the telephone every day?	_____	_____	_____
6. take care of children?	_____	_____	_____
7. sing in the shower?	_____	_____	_____
8. cook your own meals?	_____	_____	_____
9. sleep well at night?	_____	_____	_____

NEIGHBOURS

1. argue	4. bother	7. have a party	10. next door
2. baby-sit	5. friendly	8. help	11. problem
3. borrow	6. gossip	9. lend	12. unfriendly

Partner Interview

Practise these questions with your teacher. • *Then ask your partner.*

1. How many neighbours do you know?
2. Are your neighbours friendly?
3. What languages do your neighbours speak?
4. Do you visit your neighbours?
5. Do the children in your neighbourhood play together? What games do they play?
6. Do the children ever argue?
7. Do you have any problems with your neighbours? What kind of problems?

Group Role Play

Work in groups of four or five. • *Choose one scene.* • *Write a role play with your group.* • *Include roles for everyone.* • *Present your role play to the class.*

PROBLEMS AT HOME

1. cockroach
2. drip
3. exterminator
4. flooded
5. freezing
6. leak
7. leaking roof
8. mouse
9. off
10. on
11. overflow
12. pest
13. pesticide
14. plunger
15. radiator
16. shiver

Group Problem Posing/Problem Solving

Work in groups of five • State the problems. • Give advice to the people. • Suggest solutions. • Read your problems and solutions to the class.

Group Role Play

Work in groups of five. • Choose one scene. • Write a role play with your group. • Include roles for everyone. • Present your role play to the class.

Strip Stories

Discuss these stories with your class. • State the problems. • What mistakes are they making? • Write captions.

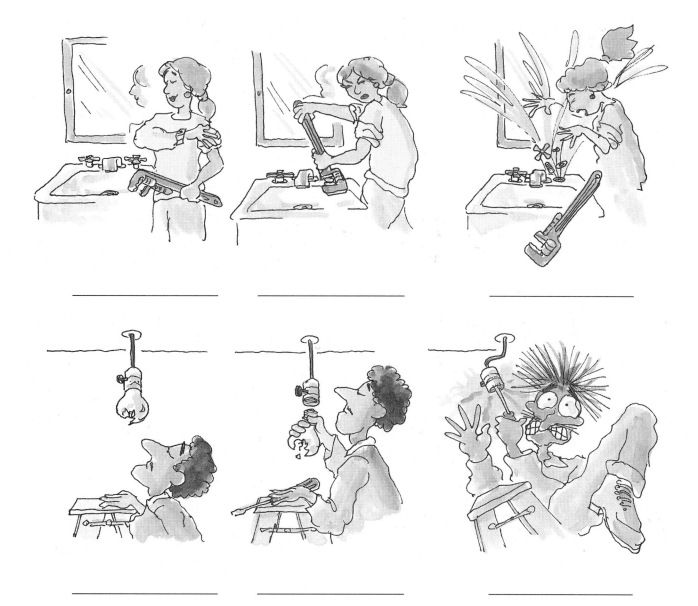

Group Activity

Work in groups of five. • Make a list of problems you have at home. • Read your list to the class. • Compare lists. • What is the biggest problem? • Make a list on the board. • Copy the new words into your notebook. • Discuss solutions for all the problems.

REVIEW

Partner Interview   Partner's name _____

Practise these questions with your teacher. • *Then ask your partner.*

1. What is today's date?
2. What is your name?
3. Where do you live?
4. How many rooms are in your home?
5. Where do you study?

6. Where do you watch TV?
7. Where do you eat breakfast?
8. Do you have neighbours?
9. Do you like your neighbours?
10. Why?

Write

Write about your partner.

Journal

_____
(1)

My partner's name is _____. My
                                        (2)

partner lives in _____ . S/he
                        (3)

has _____ rooms in his/her home. S/he
          (4)

studies in the _____
                              (5)

S/he watches TV in the_____.
                                    (6)

She/he eats breakfast in the_____.
                                      (7)

_____ _____ neighbours.
(Partner's name)   (8)

S/he _____ the neighbours because
          (9)

_____.
              (10)

Tell the Class

Read your journal to the class. • *Tell the class about your partner.*

UNIT 6

SHOPPING

GOING SHOPPING!

1. coffee shop (café)	7. mall	13. sports store
2. department store	8. men's clothing store	14. stationery store
3. electronics store	9. music store	15. toy store
4. flower shop	10. pharmacy	16. women's clothing store
5. hardware store	11. shoe store	
6. jewellery store	12. shopping centre	

Class Activity

Are these stores in your neighbourhood? • *Write the names of your neighbourhood stores on the signs.* • *What do you buy in each of the stores?* • *Make a list on the board of three items for each store.*

Group Discussion

Work in groups of five. • *Discuss these questions.* • *Report your answers to the class.*

1. Where do you shop?
2. When do you go shopping?
3. What stores do you go to?
4. Which stores in your neighbourhood do you like best? Why?
5. Which store do you recommend to the class?
6. Do you like a large department store or a small specialty shop? Can you name some?

SPORTS STORE

1. baseball	7. fishing reel	13. golf tee	19. ski boots
2. baseball bat	8. fishing rod	14. helmet	20. ski poles
3. baseball glove	9. fly	15. hockey puck	21. skis
4. basketball	10. football	16. hockey stick	22. soccer ball
5. bowling ball	11. golf ball	17. pads	23. soccer shoes
6. cleats	12. golf club	18. skates	24. sweatsuit

Class Discussion

1. What is your favourite sport?
2. Where do you buy sports equipment?
3. What do you buy?
4. Is it expensive? How much does it cost?
5. What kind of clothing do you buy in a sports store?

Group Decision

Work in groups of four. • Decide what to buy for one of the following situations. • Report your decisions to the class.

1. Your ten-year-old nephew is having a birthday. He is on a baseball team for the first time.
2. Your sister and brother-in-law are having an anniversary. Your sister likes to play golf. Your brother-in-law likes to bowl.
3. You live in a warm climate. You want to take up a new sport.

Group Vocabulary Challenge

Work in groups of four. • Make a list of special equipment you need for these sports. • Read your list to the class. • Which group had the most new words? • Make a list on the board. • Copy the list into your notebook.

skiing	baseball
golf	hockey
ice skating	basketball
bowling	other: _____

Partner Activity

Partner's name _____

Match the items. • Compare your answers with the class.

A	B
ski poles	puck
soccer ball	baseball
hockey stick	bowling shoes
baseball glove	soccer shoes
bowling ball	ski jacket

TOY STORE

1. bicycle	5. computer game	10. mobile	15. teddy bear
2. board game	6. crayons	11. model airplane	16. toy kitchen
3. books	7. doll	12. paint set	17. tricycle
4. car	8. electric train	13. rubber ball	18. truck
	9. fire engine	14. stuffed animal	

Partner Interview

Practise these questions with your teacher. • Then ask your partner.

1. When you were a child, did you have a favourite toy? What was it?
2. What children's toys were popular in your country when you were a child? What is popular now?
3. What do children like to play with in Canada?
4. Do you buy toys? Where do you buy them?

Group Decision

Work in groups of four. • Decide what toy to buy for each of these children. • Report your decisions to the class.

1. a baby girl
2. a two-year-old boy
3. an eight-year-old boy
4. a five-year-old girl
5. a ten-year-old girl

Group Survey

Ask everyone in your group these questions. • Check YES or NO. • Count the answers. • Report your group's results to the class. • Write the class' results on the board.

When you were a child:	YES	NO
1. did you ever play with dolls?	_____	_____
2. did you ever play with marbles?	_____	_____
3. did you like to colour?	_____	_____
4. did you like to play ball?	_____	_____
5. did you like to read?	_____	_____

SHOE STORE

1. baby shoes	8. length	16. rubber boots	24. walking shoes
2. canvas	9. loafers	17. sandals	25. Western boots
3. fit	10. man-made material	18. shoe horn	26. (W) wide
4. flat	11. (M) medium	19. shoe polish	27. width
5. heel	12. moccasins	20. shoe trees	28. winter boots
6. high heels	13. (N) narrow	21. slippers	29. work boots
7. leather	14. plastic	22. sole	
	15. pumps	23. suede	

Group Role Play

Work in groups of five. • Write a role play for the scene. • Include roles for everyone. • Present your role play to the class.

Find Someone Who

Review the vocabulary with your teacher. • *Fill in the name of someone who . . .*

1. _____ has more than ten pairs of shoes.
2. _____ wants cowboy boots.
3. _____ buys expensive shoes.
4. _____ wears the same size shoes as you do.
5. _____ has more than one pair of work shoes.

Group Discussion

Work in groups of five. • *Discuss these questions.* • *Report your answers to the class.*

1. How many pairs of shoes do you have?
2. Where do you buy your shoes?
3. What shoes do you wear to work?
4. What shoes do you wear to school?
5. What shoes do you wear to go dancing?
6. What kind of shoes do you wear in cold weather?
7. What kind of shoes are popular in your country?
8. Which shoes are your favourite shoes?
7. What is your shoe size?

Cross-Cultural Exchange

What kinds of shoes are popular in your country? • *Are shoe sizes in your country different from shoes sizes in Canada?* • *Are shoes made in your country?* • *What kinds?*

MEN'S CLOTHING STORE

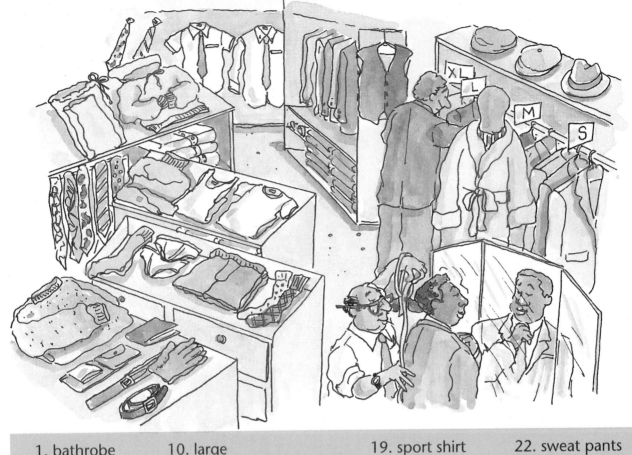

1. bathrobe	10. large	19. sport shirt	22. sweat pants
2. belts	11. long sleeves	20. suit	23. tie
3. bow-tie	12. made-to-measure	21. sweater	24. turtleneck
4. cap	13. medium	cardigan	25. tuxedo
5. dress shirt	14. pajamas	crew-neck	26. undershirt
6. extra large	15. scarf	pullover	27. windbreaker
7. gloves	16. short sleeves	vest	
8. hat	17. small	V-neck	
9. jeans	18. sport jacket		

Partner Interview

Partner's name _____

Practise these questions with your teacher. • *Then ask your partner.*

1. Where is the men's wear store in your neighbourhood?
2. What can you buy in that store?
3. When do you shop for men's clothes?
4. Who do you buy men's clothing for?

Group Decision

Work in groups of five or six. • *Decide what clothing the men in the picture will buy for the following activities.* • *Report your decisions to the class.*

1. jogging
2. a job interview
3. a wedding
4. fixing a car
5. going to a movie
6. going to class

WOMEN'S CLOTHING STORE

1. bathing suit	7. cocktail dress	13. nightgown	19. skirt	25. sweat pants
2. bathrobe	8. evening gown	14. pantyhose	20. slacks	26. sweatshirt
3. belt	9. hat	15. purse (handbag)	21. slip	27. tights
4. blazer	10. headband	16. robe	22. stockings	28. T-shirts
5. blouse	11. jeans	17. scarf	23. suit	29. underpants
6. bra(ssiere)	12. jumper	18. shorts	24. sweater	

Partner Vocabulary Challenge   Partner's name _____

Make a list of the other vocabulary words in this picture. • How many words do you remember?
• Compare your list with another pair of students. • Add to your list.

Group Decision

Work in groups of five or six. • With your group, decide what one of these women will buy for her honeymoon. • Report your decisions to the class.

   1. What is her name?
   2. Where will she go?
   3. Who will she go with?
   4. What new clothes will she buy?
   5. How much money will she spend?
   6. How will she pay for the clothes?

Community Activity

Bring in flyers and newspaper ads for women's clothing. • Choose one item to buy. • How much does it cost? • Make a list on the board of the items everyone in the class wants to buy. • List the prices. • Who wanted the most expensive item? the least expensive? • What was the most popular item? • Where do you shop for women's clothes?

DEPARTMENT STORE

1. appliance	9. gift wrap	17. parking garage
2. children's department	10. home entertainment	18. shoe department
3. cosmetics	11. home furnishings	19. sporting goods
4. customer service	12. jewellery counter	20. stationery/books
5. domestics	13. ladies' room	21. store directory
6. dressing room	14. linens	22. women's department
7. elevator	15. men's department	
8. escalator	16. men's room	

Class Discussion

1. Is there a department store in your neighbourhood? Where?
2. Do you shop there? What do you buy?
3. Which is your favourite department store? Why do you like it?
4. Are department stores the same or different in your country? Tell the class.

Partner Game: *"What do you remember?"*   **Partner's name** _____

Look at the picture with your partner. • *Remember as much as you can.* • *Close your book.* • *Describe the picture.* • *List everything.* • *Compare your list with another pair of students.* • *Add to your list.*

Partner Role Play   **Partner's name** _____

With your partner, write role plays for three of these situations. • *Present your role plays to the class.*

You are at the escalator and want to get to:

1. the gift wrap counter
2. the children's department
3. the jewellery department
4. the men's department

FLORIST

1. bouquet	7. daffodil	14. gladiola	21. philodendron
2. bud	8. daisy	15. green plant	22. pot
3. carnation	9. fern	16. iris	23. ribbon
4. chrysanthemum	10. floral arrangement	17. leaf	24. stem
or mum plant	11. florist	18. lily	25. thorn
5. corsage	12. gardenia	19. orchid	
6. crocus	13. geranium	20. petal	

What's the Story?

Work in groups of three or four. • *Tell the story of each person in the florist shop.* • *Everyone in the group should contribute at least two sentences.* • *Read your story to the class.*

1. Who are the people? What are their names?
2. What occasions are they buying flowers for?
3. What are they going to do when they leave the shop?

Partner Role Play

Partner's name _____

With your partner, choose one situation. • *Write a role play.* • *Present your conversation to the class.*

1. You are buying flowers for your 85-year-old grandmother's birthday. What do you buy? How much do you want to spend? What will you write on the card?
2. Your friend is in the hospital. You want to buy some flowers or a plant to bring when you visit. How much do you want to spend? What do you want to buy? What will you write on the card?
3. It's the last day of class. You are buying a plant for your teacher. How much money did you collect? What will you buy? Will you have the florist put a ribbon around the plant? What colour? What will you write on the card?

Class Discussion

1. What is your favourite flower? Why do you like it?
2. When do you buy flowers?
3. Is there a florist in your neighbourhood? Where? What can you buy?
4. How can you send flowers?
5. When do people give flowers and plants in your country?

PHARMACY

1. antacid	6. cough syrup	11. medicine	16. sunscreen
2. baby products	7. diapers	12. mouthwash	17. tissues
3. chapstick	8. film	13. nail polish	18. toothbrush
4. cold medicine	9. lipstick	14. prescription	19. toothpaste
5. cosmetics	10. lotion	15. shampoo	20. vitamins

Group Vocabulary Challenge

Work in groups of four or five. • Make a list of everything you buy at the pharmacy. • Compare your list with another group. • Which group had the most new words? • Make a list of new words on the board. • Copy the new words into your notebook. • Can you name a pharmacy near your home?

Class Poll

Take a poll. • Use the list on the board. • How many students buy the items at the pharmacy? • Write the total next to each item. • What do most students buy?

Conversation Squares

Work in groups of three. • First write your own answers. • Then ask your partners the questions. • Write their answers. • Compare your group's answers with other groups.

Brand	You _____	Partner 1 _____	Partner 2 _____
toothpaste	_____	_____	_____
tissue	_____	_____	_____
hand soap			
shampoo	_____	_____	_____
aspirin	_____	_____	_____
	_____	_____	_____

Community Activity

Compare the prices for the following items in two different stores. • Report the results to the class.

ITEM	STORE:_____	STORE:_____
soap: brand _____		
size: _____	Price $_____	Price $_____
shampoo: brand _____		
size: _____	Price $_____	Price $_____
toothpaste: brand _____		
size: _____	Price $_____	Price $_____
Vitamin C: brand _____		
size: _____	Price $_____	Price $_____
dose: _____		
cough syrup: brand _____		
size: _____	Price $_____	Price $_____

JEWELLERY STORE

1. bracelet	5. emerald	10. pearl	14. silver
2. chain	6. engagement ring	11. pin	15. turquoise
3. diamond	7. gold	12. ring	16. watch
4. earrings	8. jade	13. ruby	17. wedding ring
	9. necklace		

Group Role Play

Work in groups of three. • Choose one pair of people in the jewellery store. • Write a role play.
• Include roles for everyone. • Present your role play to the class.

Partner Interview   Partner's name _____

Practise these questions with your teacher. • Then ask your partner.

1. Do you wear any jewellery? What do you wear?
2. What jewellery are you wearing today?
3. Do you ever buy jewellery? Who do you buy jewellery for?
4. Did you ever receive jewellery for a present? What did you get?
5. Can you name a jewellery store in your neighbourhood?

HARDWARE STORE

1. bolts	8. hammer	15. nuts	22. power saw	29. tool
2. chisel	9. handsaw	16. paint	23. sandpaper	30. tool box
3. crowbar	10. hatchet	17. paintbrush	24. screw driver	31. turpentine
4. electrical tape	11. key	18. paint can	25. screws	32. vise
5. electric drill	12. level	19. plane	26. stepladder	33. washer
6. glue	13. lock	20. pliers	27. switch	34. wire
7. glue gun	14. nails	21. plunger	28. tape measure	35. wrench

Class Discussion

1. Do you ever go to the hardware store?
2. Which one?
3. What do you buy?
4. How are the prices?

Partner Activity

Partner's name _____

Decide what is happening in the picture. • Report your answers to the class:

1. What is the man going to do with the ladder?
2. Why is the woman making a duplicate key?
3. What is the woman buying at the cash register?
4. What will the couple use the paint for? What colour will they choose?

Class Game: *"Mime"*

Pantomime using a tool. • Whoever guesses the tool takes the next turn.

OFFICE SUPPLY STORE

1. computer paper	8. manila folder	16. rubber cement
2. correction fluid	9. masking tape	17. rulers
3. desk calendar	10. notebooks	18. stapler
4. envelope	11. paper	19. staples
5. file cabinet	12. paper clip	20. tape
6. glue	13. pencils	21. typewriter ribbon
7. greeting card	14. pens	22. typing paper
	15. rubber band	

Class Discussion

What do you use these supplies for? Do you know the name of an office supply store?

Find Someone Who

Review the vocabulary with your teacher. • *Fill in the name of someone who . . .*

1. _____ can type.
2. _____ can change a typewriter ribbon.
3. _____ can use a fax machine.
4. _____ has a desk calendar.
5. _____ can use a copy machine.

Group Activity

Work in groups of four or five. • *Put the supplies you have with you on the desk.* • *Make a list of what your group has.* • *Compare your list with the class.*

ELECTRONICS STORE

1. adding machine	10. CD (compact disc)	19. monitor
2. answering	11. colour TV	20. personal computer
3. audio cassettes	12. computer keyboard	21. printer
4. black & white TV	13. cordless phone	22. short wave radio
5. boombox	14. fax machine	23. tape deck
6. calculator	15. floppy disk	24. telephone cord
7. camcorder	16. headphones	25. telephone jack
8. car radio	17. modem	26. turntable
9. cassette recorder	18. modular telephone	27. videotape

Group Decision

Work in groups of five or six. • Decide on the best prices for the items in the illustration. • Write prices on the tags. • Compare your prices with the class.

Class Discussion

1. What electronic equipment do you have?
2. What do you want?
3. What equipment do you like to use?
4. Do you use any of this equipment at work? What do you use?
5. What kind of equipment is popular in your country? What do people have in their homes?

SALES AND ADVERTISEMENTS

1. clearance	4. final sale	7. limited quantity	10. sale price
2. damaged goods	5. garage sale	8. regular price	11. seconds
3. end of season	6. inventory	9. return policy	12. white sale

Strip Stories

Discuss these stories with your class. • Did you ever have any of these experiences? • Tell the class.

Advertisements

Read these two ads and discuss them with your class. Are they good sales?

(Look for the regular price.)

(See if the sale is on first quality merchandise or seconds [damaged merchandise].)

Pictures for Conversation: Sales

What is happening in these pictures? Did you ever have a problem with a sale?

Group Discussion

Work in groups of five. • *Discuss these questions.* • *Report your answers to the class.*

1. What kind of sales are these?
2. Do you like to shop at sales like these?
3. What have you bought on a sale?
4. Is there a good sale now? Where?
5. What store in your community has the best sale?
6. When do you have to be careful when you buy on sale?

Community Activity

Bring in flyers for sales to class. • *What do you want to buy?* • *How much money can you save?*

111

REVIEW

Group Decision

Work in groups of five. • Your group has $1,000. • Decide how to spend it. • You can buy something together or divide the money. • If you divide it, each person decides how to spend his/her portion. • Report your decisions to the class. • Remember to tell:

1. what you will buy
2. where you will buy it
3. who you will buy it for
4. when you will buy it
5. what you will do with it

Partner Writing Activity

Partner's name _____

Ask your partner these questions. • Then write a paragraph about your partner. • Read your paragraph to your partner. • Read it to the class.

1. Is money important to you? Why?
2. Do you ever save money?
3. What do you like to spend money on?
4. What don't you like to spend money on?
5. If you won the lottery, what would you do with the money?

Speech

Tell the class about your favourite store. • Include everything you like about the store. • Show the class something you bought there.

UNIT 7

YOUR NEIGHBOURHOOD

1. convenience store	7. newspaper store	13. stickball
2. garbage can	8. parking meter	14. stoop
3. ice cream truck	9. parking space	15. street corner
4. laundromat	10. pizza shop	16. traffic
5. mailbox	11. recycling bin	17. traffic light
6. neighbour	12. shoemaker	18. urban

Class Discussion

1. Do you like your neighbourhood? How long have you been living there?
2. Is there a traffic light on your street? Where is it?
3. Does the ice cream truck come to your neighbourhood? When?
4. Do children play in the street in your neighbourhood? What do they play?
5. Where do people walk their dogs in your neighbourhood?

Find Someone Who

Review the vocabulary with your teacher. Fill in the name of someone who . . .

1. _____ lives near a playground.
2. _____ lives near a mailbox.
3. _____ lives near a store.
4. _____ recycles paper.
5. _____ recycles cans and bottles.

YOUR COMMUNITY

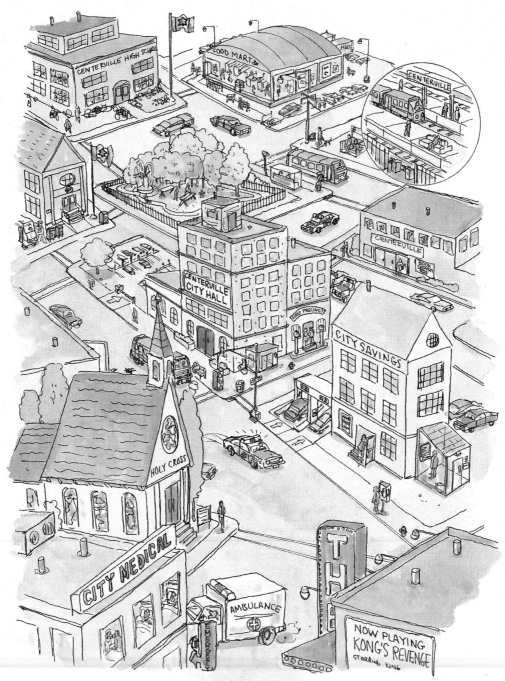

1. bank	10. school	19. in front of
2. church	11. supermarket	20. just before
3. city hall	12. bus	21. just past
4. hospital	13. subway	22. next to
5. library	14. taxi	23. on the corner
6. movie theatre	15. train	24. straight ahead
7. parking lot	16. across from	25. turn right (left)
8. post office	17. behind	26. (two) blocks
9. public phone	18. between	27. opposite

Class Discussion

1. Does your city look like this? What buildings do you recognize?
2. Do you go to the library? Does the library have a foreign book section? What languages? Do you have a library card?
3. When do you go to the post office? What do you ask for? Do you ever have problems there?
4. Is there a bank in your community? Do you use it? When? What do you do there?
5. Is there public transportation in your community? Is it good? Do you use it? When do you use it?

Partner Role Play   Partner's name _____

Complete these conversations. • Use the map on page 116. • Present your conversations to the class.

1. At City Hall

A: Excuse me. How can I get to the post office?

B: _____

A: Thank you.

2. At the Bank

A: Excuse me. Can you tell me how to get to the library?

B: _____

A: Thanks.

3. At the Movie Theatre

A: Pardon me. Could you please tell me where I can park my car?

B. _____

A: Thanks very much.

4. At the Library

A: Pardon me. Do you know where I can make a phone call?

B: _____

A: Thanks a lot.

5. At the Subway Station

A: Say. Can you tell me where the school is?

B: _____

A: Thank you.

THE TELEPHONE

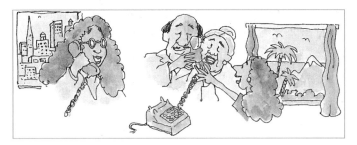

1. answering machine	7. hang up	13. receiver
2. busy signal	8. hold	14. telephone call
3. cellular phone	9. local call	15. telephone number
4. cord	10. long distance	16. touch tone
5. cordless	11. message	17. wrong number
6. directory assistance	12. operator	18. 800 number

Class Discussion

What is happening in these pictures?

Partner Interview

Partner's name _____

Practise these questions with your teacher. • *Then ask your partner.*

1. What is your telephone number?
2. What is your area code?
3. What kind of telephone do you have?
4. Do you make a lot of long distance calls? Where do you call?
5. Who do you call most often?

Cross-Cultural Exchange

What are telephones like in your country? • *How do you make a long distance call?* • *Do many people have telephones in their homes?*

Partner Role Play

Partner's name _____

Complete these phone conversations. • *Present one to the class.*

1. **Answering machine**

   Machine: I'm not here right now. Please leave a message at the tone. BEEEEEP

   You:_____

2. **Wrong number**

   Stranger: Hello.

   You: Hello. This is_____. Is_____ there?

   Stranger: _____

   You: _____

3. **Long distance directory assistance**

   Operator: What city?

   You: _____

   Operator: What name?

   You: I'd like the number for _____

   Operator: Please hold for the number:

   (or) The number is: _____

Partner Role Play

Partner's name _____

Decide what to say for these phone calls. • *Present one conversation to the class.*

1. local directory assistance for the number of your school
2. your school when you can't come to class
3. the landlord when your roof is leaking
4. the drug store when you need to know their hours
5. the telephone company when your bill is incorrect

Community Activity

Use your local telephone directory. • *Find the names, addresses, and telephone numbers.*

LOOK UP	NAME	ADDRESS	TELEPHONE NUMBER
1. a drugstore	_____	_____	_____
2. a movie theatre	_____	_____	_____
3. a restaurant	_____	_____	_____
4. a plumber	_____	_____	_____
5. a place of worship	_____	_____	_____
6. your school	_____	_____	_____
7. a hospital	_____	_____	_____
8. the telephone company business office	_____	_____	_____
9. local directory assistance		_____	_____
10. long distance directory assistance		_____	_____
11. a travel agency	_____	_____	_____
12. a dentist	_____	_____	_____

Circle Dialogue

Do a circle dialogue with the question, "When do you call a ...?" • *Continue around the circle.*

Teacher: "When do you call a plumber?"

Student 1: "I call a plumber when my sink is broken. When do you call a tire store?"

Student 2: "I call a tire store when I need information about tires. When do you call ...?"

USING THE TELEPHONE

These instructions are not in the correct sequence. Read the instructions and number them in the correct order, 1 to 6.

_____ Dial the number you want.

_____ Put a coin in the slot.

_____ When you finish your call, hang up the receiver.

_____ Take the receiver off the hook.

_____ If there is no answer, hang up and get your coin back from the change return.

_____ Wait for the dial tone.

Practise saying these telephone numbers.

1. 555-1212   <u>five five five one two one two</u>

2. 435-8300   <u>four three five eight three hundred (or three oh oh)**</u>

3. 326-8000   <u>three two six eight thousand (or eight oh oh oh)</u>

4. 927-8200   _____

5. 602-914-2000   _____

6. 716-659-8600   _____

---

*   *A local call is a call to the same city or a city close to the one you are calling from.*

** *Zero is usually called "oh" on the telephone, except when two or three zeroes come together. See numbers 2 and 3 of this exercise.*

EMERGENCY: FIRE!

1. ambulance	6. fire hydrant	11. smoke
2. ax	7. hook	12. stretcher
3. burn	8. hose	13. victim
4. fire escape	9. paramedic	
5. fire fighter	10. siren	

Class Discussion

What is happening? • What do you think caused the fire? • How can fires be prevented?

What's the Story?

Work in groups of four. • *Choose one person in the picture.* • *Tell that person's story.* • *Everyone in the group should contribute at least one sentence.* • *Read your story to the class.*

1. What is his/her name?
2. Why is he/she at the fire scene?
3. What is he/she doing?
4. What will happen next?

Group Discussion

Work in groups of four. • *Discuss these questions.* • *Report your answers to the class.*

1. Have you ever seen a fire? What happened?
2. Are you afraid of fire? Why or why not?
3. Did you play with fire when you were a child? What did you do?
4. Are fires a problem in your country? Why or why not?
5. Tell the most interesting story to the class.

Partner Role Play   Partner's name _____

Write a conversation to report a fire to the 911 emergency operator. • *Present your conversation to the class.*

911 Operator: _____

You: _____

911 Operator: _____

You: _____

911 Operator: _____

You: _____

EMERGENCY: POLICE!

1. arrest	5. crime	9. hubcap	13. report
2. break	6. danger	10. owner	14. steal
3. break in	7. freeze!	11. police	15. thief
4. carjack	8. handcuffs	12. police car	16. witness

Strip Story

What is happening? • Fill in the bubbles. • Discuss this story with your class.

124

Group Decision

Work in groups of four. • *What should you do in these emergencies?* • *Decide with your group.*
• *Report your decisions to the class.*

Partner Activity

Partner's name _____

Choose one emergency. • *Write a conversation between the 911 operator and yourself.* •
Present your conversation to the class.

1. Who are you?
2. Where are you?
3. What happened?
4. When did it happen?
5. Is anyone hurt?
6. What should you do while you wait?

THE POST OFFICE

1. air mail	5. insurance	9. package	13. scale
2. counter	6. letter	10. parcel post	14. stamp
3. envelope	7. mail	11. post card	15. stamp machine
4. first class	8. mail truck	12. postal worker	16. third class

Class Discussion

What is happening in the picture?

Class Game: *"What do you remember?"*

Look at the picture. • Remember as much as you can. • Close your book. • List everything. • Compare your answers with your class. • Who had the longest list? • Open your book and check your answers.

Partner Activity

Partner's name_____

Choose a person from the line in the picture. • *Write a paragraph and read it to the class.*
1. What is the person's name?
2. What is he/she doing at the post office?
3. What will he/she say when it is his/her turn?
4. Where is the letter or package going?
5. Who will receive it?

Partner Role Play

Partner's name_____

Write a conversation for you and a postal clerk. • *Present your conversation to the class.*
1. What do you want at the post office?
2. What will the clerk say to you?
3. What will you say to the clerk?
4. How much money will you need?

Partner Interview

Partner's name_____

Practise these questions with your teacher. • *Then ask your partner.*
1. Do you like to write letters?
2. How often do you write letters?
3. Who do you write to?
4. How often do you receive letters?
5. How often do you go to the post office?
6. What do you do there?

Group Problem Posing/Problem Solving

Work in groups of three. • *State the problem.* • *Find a solution.* • *Report your decisions to the class.*

You wait in line for ten minutes in the post office. You buy stamps and some post cards for $12.80. You give the clerk a $50.00 bill. The clerk gives you $7.20 in change. What will you say to the clerk?

THE BANK

1. account	8. credit card	16. PIN number
2. ATM	9. deposit slip	(personal
(automated teller	10. loan application	identification number)
machine)	11. money order	17. safety deposit box
3. bank	12. monthly statement	18. save
4. bank officer	13. overdraw	19. savings account
5. cash	14. payroll cheque	20. teller
6. change	15. personal cheque	21. travellers' cheque
7. chequing account		22. withdrawal slip

Class Activity

What are the people doing in the bank? • *Make a list on the board of everything they are doing.*

Class Discussion

1. What is the name of the closest bank to your home? Where is it?
2. Do you use the bank?
3. When do you go to the bank?
4. Do you have a savings account? a chequing account?
5. What are some things you can put in the safety deposit box?

Work in groups of three. • State the problems. • Find solutions. • Report your decisions to the class. • Present a role play about one of these problems.

This woman works in a bank. She's a teller. You are cashing a cheque for $50 and she gives you $60. What do you say? What will she do?

This man is a bank robber. He is robbing the bank. What will the teller do? What will the robber do? What should you do if you are there?

This man overdrew his account. What will he do? What should you do if you overdraw your account?

PUBLIC TRANSPORTATION

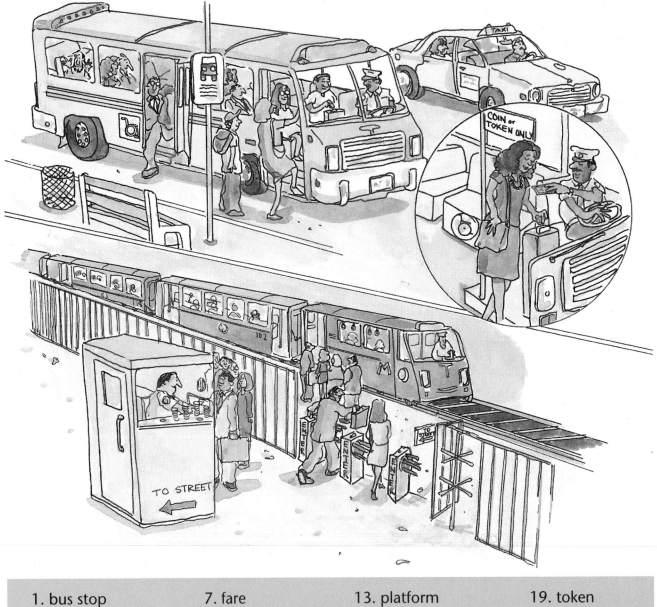

1. bus stop	7. fare	13. platform	19. token
2. cab	8. front	14. rear	20. transfer
3. driver	9. front door	15. rear door	21. turnstile
4. entrance	10. get off	16. seat	22. wait
5. exact change	11. get on	17. subway/metro	
6. exit	12. passenger	18. taxi driver	

Class Discussion

1. What kind of public transportation do you have in your community?
2. Do you use it? When?
3. How much is the bus fare? The subway fare?
4. Is it crowded? When is it most crowded?
5. Do you get on at the front or in the rear? Where do you get off?
6. What do you say if you want to get off?
7. Is it safe? When is it dangerous? Why is it dangerous?

Group Role Play

Work in groups of three. • *Write a conversation between the taxi driver and the two passengers.* • *Include roles for everyone.* • *Present your conversation to the class.*

Group Problem Posing/Problem Solving

Work in groups of three. • *State the problems.* • *Find solutions.* • *Report your decisions to the class.*

1. You take the bus to school on the first day of class. After two stops, you realize you are on the wrong bus.
2. You are in a subway station with two friends, waiting for the train. The train comes. You get on, but the door closes too fast. Your friends are still in the station.
3. You get on the bus. After the bus starts, you realize you don't have exact change.

Group Survey

Ask everyone in your group these questions. • *Check the kinds of transportation and advantages.* • *Count your answers.* • *Report your group's results to the class.* • *Write the class' results on the board.*

	ADVANTAGES			
TRANSPORTATION	Cheap	Convenient	Fast	Safe
bus	___	___	___	___
train	___	___	___	___
taxi	___	___	___	___
private car	___	___	___	___
bicycle	___	___	___	___
feet	___	___	___	___

YOUR CAR

1. accelerator (gas pedal)
2. baby seat
3. brake
4. bumper
5. car key
6. clutch
7. emergency brake
8. exhaust pipe
9. headlight
10. fender
11. fuel gauge

12. gas cap
13. gear shift
14. glove compartment
15. hood
16. hub cap
17. ignition
18. licence plate
19. odometer
20. rear view mirror
21. seat belt
22. side view mirror

23. signal light
24. speedometer
25. steering wheel
26. tail light
27. temperature gauge
28. trunk
29. wheel
30. windshield
31. windshield wiper

Partner Interview

Partner's name _____

Practise these questions with your teacher. • *Then ask your partner.*

1. Do you have a driver's licence?
2. Do you drive a standard shift? an automatic?
3. Do you have a car? What kind?
4. What kind of car would you like to drive?
5. What is the most popular car in your country?

TRAFFIC AND ROAD SIGNS

Vocabulary

Have you ever seen these signs? What do they mean? Match the vocabulary with the signs.

1. No parking
2. Railroad crossing
3. Do not enter
4. One-way street
5. Do not exceed 50 km/h
6. School zone ahead
7. Pedestrian crossing
8. No U-turn

Community Activity

Which of these signs are in your neighbourhood? • What colour is each sign? • Draw the signs in your neighbourhood. • Note the colours. • Bring your signs to class. • What do they say? • What do the colours signify?

THE GAS STATION

1. air	6. gas pump	11. lift	16. self service
2. attendant	7. high test	12. litre	17. tire
3. engine	8. inspection	13. oil	18. unleaded
4. full service	9. leaded	14. radiator	19. windshield washer fluid
5. gasoline	10. lever	15. repairs	

Partner Activity

Partner's name _____

Decide what to say. • *Present your answers to the class.*

1. you want the attendant to check your oil
2. you want $10 worth of premium gasoline
3. you have a flat tire and need some help
4. you need your car inspected

Group Vocabulary Challenge

Work in groups of four or five. • *Make a list of vocabulary words about cars and gas stations.* • *Compare your list with another group.* • *Which group had the most new words?* • *Make a list on the board.* • *Copy the new words into your notebook.*

THE LAUNDROMAT AND DRY CLEANER'S

1. bleach	7. dry cleaner	13. rinse cycle	19. wash cycle
2. clean	8. fabric softener	14. sort	20. washing machine
3. cold water	9. hanger	15. spin cycle	21. white wash
4. dark wash	10. hot water	16. spot	
5. detergent	11. load	17. starch	
6. dirty	12. press	18. warm water	

Partner Game: *"What do you remember?"*   Partner's name _____

Look at the picture with your partner. • Remember as much as you can. • Close your book. • Describe the picture with your partner. • List everything. • Compare your list with another pair of students. • Add to your list.

What's the Story?

Work in groups of five. • Write a story about the scene in the laundromat. • Everyone in the group should contribute at least two sentences. • Use these questions or make up your own. • Read your story to the class.

1. Who are the people?
2. What are their names?
3. What day is it?
4. What time is it?
5. What will happen between the man and the woman?

REVIEW

Speech

Choose a topic and explain it to the class:

1. How do you ride a bus?
2. How do you get gas at a self-service station?
3. How do you wash clothes at the laundromat?
4. How do you call directory assistance?
5. How do you buy stamps at the post office?
6. How do you report a fire emergency?

Partner Vocabulary Challenge

Partner's name _____

Make lists to answer each question. • Read your list to the class.

1. What do people do at the bank?
2. What do people do at the post office?
3. What emergencies do people call 911 for?
4. What do people do at the gas station?
5. What do people do at the dry cleaners?

Community Activity

Draw a map from your school to your house. • Explain your map to your class.

UNIT 8

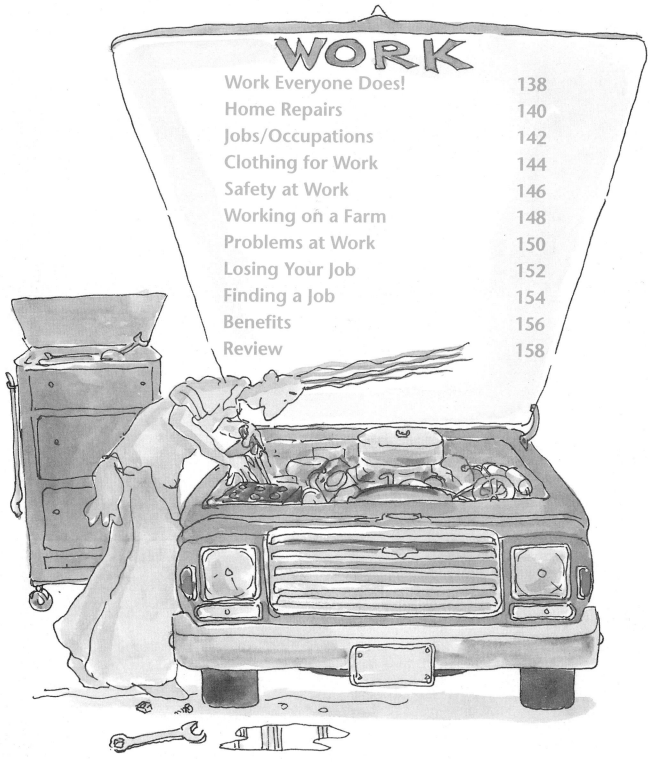

WORK

WORK EVERYONE DOES!

1. burned out	6. dust the furniture	11. iron clothes
2. change the light bulb	7. feed the dog	12. rake the leaves
3. clean (the refrigerator)	8. fold clean clothes	13. vacuum
4. cook	9. defrost the freezer	14. wash the windows
5. dry the dishes	10. hammer a nail	

Group Survey

Ask everyone in your group these questions. • *Check EVERY DAY/OFTEN/OCCASIONALLY/NEVER.* • *Count your answers.* • *Report your group's results to the class.* • *Write the class' results on the board.*

How often do you:	EVERY DAY	OFTEN	OCCASIONALLY	NEVER
1. cook?	_____	_____	_____	_____
2. change a light bulb?	_____	_____	_____	_____
3. wash the dishes?	_____	_____	_____	_____
4. hammer a nail?	_____	_____	_____	_____
5. paint the house?	_____	_____	_____	_____
6. dust the furniture?	_____	_____	_____	_____
7. rake the leaves?	_____	_____	_____	_____

Class Game: *"Test your memory"*

Close your book. • Listen to your teacher tell the story. • Open your book. • Write the correct order in the boxes. • Read your story to the class in the correct order.

Cross-Cultural Exchange

Who does the housework in your home? • In your country, do men help with housework? • Should men help with housework? • Why or why not? • What electric appliances do people use to do housework in your country?

139

HOME REPAIRS

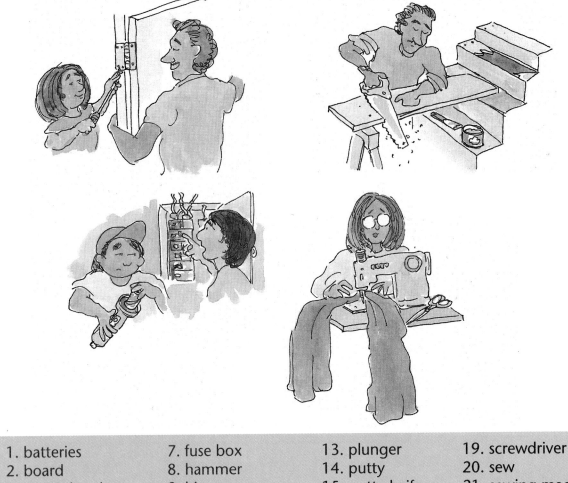

1. batteries	7. fuse box	13. plunger	19. screwdriver
2. board	8. hammer	14. putty	20. sew
3. circuit breaker	9. hinge	15. putty knife	21. sewing machine
4. drill	10. material/cloth	16. saw	22. thread
5. flashlight	11. needle	17. scissors	23. wrench
6. fuse	12. pliers	18. screw	

Class Activity

Make a list on the board of what home repairs these people are making. • *What tools are they using?* • *Copy the list into your notebook.*

Group Decision

Work in groups of five. • *Decide what to do for each situation.* • *Report your decisions to the class.*

1. The sink is clogged in the bathroom.
2. Your daughter dropped a gold ring down the toilet.
3. The lights went out in the house.
4. There is a small hole in the wall of the living room.
5. A shelf fell down from the wall.
6. The roof leaks.
7. You break a window at home.
8. Your refrigerator doesn't work.
9. You have no hot water.
10. Your kitchen tap is dripping.

What's the Story?

Work in groups of five. • *Choose one of the pictures and write a story.* • *Everyone in the group should contribute at least two sentences.* • *Read your story to the class.*

Answer these questions:

1. Who?
2. What?
3. Where?
4. When?
5. Why?

JOBS/OCCUPATIONS

1. barber	8. engineer	15. mechanic
2. carpenter	9. factory worker	16. nurse
3. chef	10. farm worker	17. police officer
4. clerk	11. fire fighter	18. secretary
5. construction worker	12. fisherman	19. teacher aide
6. dentist	13. lawyer	20. full time
7. doctor	14. manicurist	21. part time

Class Discussion

Where do these people work? • What do they do?

Group Activity

Work in groups of five. • Fill in the chart with your group. • Compare your answers with another group. • Report your answers to the class.

WHO?	WHAT?	WHERE?
1. farm worker	picks crops	on a farm
2. teacher	teaches	in a school
3. factory worker		
4. cook		
5. manicurist		
6. secretary		
7. barber		
8. hospital aide		
9. mechanic		
10. salesperson		
11. security guard		
12. taxi driver		

Group Activity

Work in groups of five. • *Decide with your group what jobs these people have.* • *Write the job title.* • *Report your decision to the class.*

1._____

2._____

3._____

4._____

Partner Role Play

Partner's name _____

A TV host is interviewing you. • *Choose a job.* • *Write a conversation between the TV host and yourself.* • *Present your role play to the class.*

1. Where do you work?
2. What is your job?
3. What hours do you work?

4. Do you like your job?
5. What job do you want in the future ?

CLOTHING FOR WORK

JOB	CLOTHING/EQUIPMENT
1. astronaut	9. badge
2. ballet dancer	10. hat
3. butcher	11. lab coat
4. custodian	12. night stick
5. lab technician	13. space suit
6. lifeguard	14. uniform
7. nurse	15. whistle
8. police officer	16. work clothes

Class Discussion

1. What work do these people do?
2. Why do they wear uniforms or costumes?
3. Who pays for the uniforms?
4. Which uniforms do you like? Why?
5. Which uniforms require special shoes? special hats? special gloves?

Group Discussion

Work in groups of four. • Look at the pictures. • Discuss these questions. • Report your opinions to the class.

1. What are the people wearing?
2. What are their jobs?

3. Are they dressed appropriately?
4. What do you wear to work?

Cross-Cultural Exchange

In your country, do work clothes look like this? • Which are the same? • Which are different?

SAFETY AT WORK

1. assembly line
2. blow torch
3. co-worker
4. foreman
5. machine
6. plant
7. safety glasses
8. safety gloves
9. safety violation
10. steel-tipped shoes
11. supervisor

Class Discussion

1. What is happening in this picture?
2. What jobs do the people have?
3. Do you think anyone is a supervisor? Which one(s)?
4. Are there any safety violations in the factory? What are the violations?
5. What kind of factory do you think it is?

Group Decision

Work in groups of five. • Decide what the people are saying. • Fill in the bubbles. • Compare your bubbles with the class.

Class Discussion

What do these signs mean? • Where do you see these signs?

Group Role Play

Work in groups of four or five. • Choose one of these situations. • Write a role play. • Include roles for everyone. • Present your conversation to the class.

1. You are new on the job. You are unsure of what to do. Ask your co-workers. When no one knows for sure, check with your supervisor.
2. It's Friday afternoon. You are taking a break. Several co-workers are sitting in the lounge having coffee and snacks. Have a conversation.

Community Activity

Are there any signs in the school building? • What do they say? • Do you notice any signs at your job? • Copy them and bring them to class. • Look for signs in other buildings. • Copy the signs. • Show the signs to the class. • Who can guess where the sign is from?

WORKING ON A FARM

1. barn	8. cow	15. goose	22. pond
2. barnyard	9. duck	16. gosling	23. ram
3. boar	10. duckling	17. hen	24. rooster
4. bull	11. ewe	18. lamb	25. sheep
5. calf	12. fence	19. mare	26. silo
6. chick	13. field	20. pig	27. sow
7. corral	14. foal	21. piglet	28. stallion

Cross-Cultural Exchange

What do these animals "say" in your native language? • *Fill in the chart.*

ANIMAL	ENGLISH	YOUR LANGUAGE
1. cat	meow	_____
2. dog	bow wow	_____
3. cow	moo	_____
4. rooster	cock-a-doodle-doo	_____
5. hen	cluck-cluck	_____
6. horse	neigh	_____
7. pig	oink	_____
8. duck	quack	_____

1. bucket	4. field	7. orchard	10. plough	13. tractor
2. clippers	5. hay	8. pick apples	11. rope	14. trough
3. corn	6. milking machine	9. pitchfork	12. shear	15. wool

Class Discussion

What is happening in these pictures? • What other work do people do on farms and ranches?

Partner Activity

Partner's name _____

Which word doesn't belong? • *Cross out the word.* • *Report your answers to the class.*

1. sheep	wool	clipper	goggles
2. barn	milk	saw	cow
3. orchard	iron	crop	harvest
4. pitchfork	grass	hay	dog
5. trough	saddle	apples	horse
6. ladder	hatchet	bucket	rooster

PROBLEMS AT WORK

1. appropriate
2. boss
3. company time
4. discrimination

5. employee
6. employer
7. excuse
8. lazy

9. personal problem
10. (sexual) harassment
11. understanding

Class Discussion

What is happening in each of these pictures? • Discuss the problems together.

Group Problem Posing/Problem Solving

Work in groups of four. • State the problems. • Pick one problem. • Find a solution. • Role play the problem and the solution for the class.

Conversation Squares

Work in groups of three. • First write your own answers • Then ask your partners the questions. • Write their answers. • Compare your group's answers with other groups.

Problem	You_____	Partner 1_____	Partner 2_____
1. What was it?	_____	_____	_____
2. How long did it last?	_____	_____	_____
3. What was the solution?	_____	_____	_____
4. Who helped you?	_____	_____	_____

LOSING YOUR JOB

1. close down	4. lay off	8. poor performance	12. temporary
2. destroy	5. manager	9. quit	13. unemployed
3. fire	6. migrant work	10. seasonal work	
	7. out of work	11. slow down	

Strip Stories

Discuss these stories with the class. • *Decide what is happening.* • *Write captions.*

Find Someone Who

Review the vocabulary with your teacher. • *Fill in the name of someone who . . .*

1. _____ has been laid off.
2. _____ has quit a job.
3. _____ has kept a bad job.
4. _____ has left a good job.
5. _____ has had seasonal work.

Group Activity

Work in groups of three. • *Answer these questions.* • *Compare your answers with others in the class.*

1. What are good reasons to quit a job?
   _____
   _____

2. What are good reasons to keep a job?
   _____
   _____

3. What are good reasons to fire an employee?
   _____
   _____

FINDING A JOB

WANT ADS

TRUCK LOADER
Moving truck loader PT work which will turn in to FT for right person. Willing to work all 3 shifts. This person should be strong, not afraid to work. Salary based on performance . APPLY AT PINE WORKS FURNITURE 3945 Adelaide, across from Post Office.

SECURITY OFFICERS
F/T or P/T exp. preferred but not mandatory Will train. Progressive wages. Must be 21 or older, have home telephone and reliable transportation. Apply in person at SECURITY SERVICES, 4455 Park Avenue, 555-3056. Women encouraged to apply. $400/week.

COURIER
For busy route. Halifax area. Good driving record a must. Call Pat. 555-4956. Mon.-Fri. $8/hr.

COUNTER POSITION
Part time. Apply in person at DayTime Dry Cleaners. 354 River St.

LE CHATEAU
Seeking qualified individuals for the following positions:

HOUSEKEEPERS
We offer:
• health benefits
• paid time off
• mileage incentive program
Please apply in person:
Le Chateau Hotel
3 Chateau Drive
Banff, Alta.
555-3956.

DENTAL RECEPTIONIST
Bilingual; Work w/great team. P/T. 1:30-6:30 p.m. Mon.-Fri. Some Sat. Will train mature person w/good people skills. Apply 345 Rosewood Ave. $15,000

NURSE ASSISTANTS:
A BRIGHT FUTURE WAITS FOR YOU. Health Care Associates has staffing opportunities for Nurse Assistants. Put your valuable skills to work in area hospitals and nursing homes. Health Care Associates offers:
• a chance to design a work schedule that works for you

• competitive pay
• the support of a highly respected, professional organization
Call Jill for more information. 555-5676

BRIGHTEN YOUR FUTURE WITH HEALTH CARE!
Adult Home Care needs responsible experienced person for all shifts. Must have own transportation. Call 555-3455.

WECARE CAR WASH
needs full time and part time help. Apply in person. Bayview & Finch.

DIRECTOR OF PUBLIC RELATIONS WANTED
Resp. incl. promotional & community relations efforts. College or graduate degree in Public Relations and/or work exp. in field. Strong written & verbal communications skills. Eng/ Fr speaker desirable. Up to $30,000. For complete description, call Marie: 555-3029 or mail resume:
MUSEUM OF INTERNATIONAL ARTS, 245 Grand Avenue, Ottawa K2B 1T4.

CASHIER - Permanent. Pharmacy experience pref. Must be reliable. Benefits. Will consider college students. Call 555-0034.

SCHOOLS & INSTRUCTION

BANK TRAINING
in 4 to 15 weeks. Financial aid if qualified. Job placement assistance. Day or evening classes. Call 555-5678.

BE A DOG GROOMER!
18 week course! Hands on training. Financial aid if qualified. Call now for information! 555-6554, Pedigree Career Institute.

GET A CAREER IN GEAR!
Auto/Diesel Technology Associate Degree Program. Financial Aid Assistance if qualified. ADC Technical and Trade School. 12 Technical Drive. 555-2345.

Class Discussion

1. Where do you think these ads are from? Have you ever seen ads like these?
2. Did you ever apply for a job through a newspaper ad? When? What kind of job was it?
3. What information do you look for in an ad?
4. When do you apply for a job through an ad?
5. Which one of these jobs in the newspaper ads interests you? Why?

Write

Fill out this employment application. • *Use it in the role play below.*

Date: _____ _____ _____
      (Month)   (Day)   (Year)

Name: _____
        (First)   (Middle Initial)   (Last)

Social Insurance Number: _____

Address: _____
      (Number)   (Street)   (Apartment)

_____
    (City)   (Province)   (Postal Code)

Telephone: (_____) - _____
     (Area Code)

Job Applying For: _____

Work Experience: _____

_____

_____

_____

Education: _____

_____

_____

_____

Partner Role Play

Partner's name _____

Choose a job from the ads. • *One partner is the applicant.* • *One is the interviewer.* • *Present your conversation to the class.*

Applicant: *ask some of these questions (or others):*
1. "What are the responsibilities of the job?"
2. "What are the hours?"
3. "Do I have to wear a uniform? Does the company provide the uniform?"
4. "What is the salary?"
5. "What are the company benefits? What am I eligible for?"

Interviewer: *ask some of these questions (or others):*
1. "Why are you interested in this job?"
2. "Why are you thinking of leaving your present job?"
3. "Do you have any experience for this job?"
4. "Can you read and write English?"
5. "Can you work overtime?"

BENEFITS

1. disability	6. retirement
2. hospitalization	7. sick day
3. maternity leave	8. unemployment insurance
4. paid holidays	9. vacation
5. pension	10. workers' compensation

Class Discussion

Which of these benefits are most important to you? • Which benefits do you have in your present job?

Group Discussion

Work in groups of five or six. • *Discuss these questions.* • *Report your answers to the class.*

1. When do you take a sick day?
2. What do you do on your vacation?
3. What days are paid holidays?
4. What do you want to do when you retire?
5. What is "maternity leave?"
6. When does a worker qualify for workers' compensation?

Group Vocabulary Challenge

Work in groups of five or six. • *Make a list of the reasons to take a sick day.* • *Read your list to the class.* • *Which group had the most new words?* • *Make a list on the board.* • *Copy the new words into your notebook.*

Class Game: *"What do you want to do on your next vacation?"*

Think. • *Write.* • *Fold.* • *Make a pile of papers.* • *Choose one.* • *Guess who wrote it.*

Group Problem Posing/Problem Solving

Work in groups of five or six. • *State this man's problem in one or two sentences.* • *Find a solution.* • *Compare your decisions with another group.*

Cross-Cultural Exchange

What benefits do employees usually get in your country? • *What is deducted from employees' paycheques?*

REVIEW

Partner's name _____

Ask your partner.

1. Where do you work?
2. What is your job?
3. What do you wear to work?
4. Do you work part time or full time?
5. When do you work?

6. Do you like your job?
7. Why or why not?
8. What is your boss like?
9. What do you want in the future?

Write

Write about your job.

Journal

I work at _____. My
(1)

job is _____. I wear _____ to
(2)   (3)

work. I work _____ and I work _____.
(4)   (5)

I _____ my job because it _____.
(6)   (7)

My boss is _____.
(8)

Someday, I want to work as _____.
(9)

Tell Your Partner

Read your journal entry to your partner. • *Listen to your partner's journal.*

UNIT 9

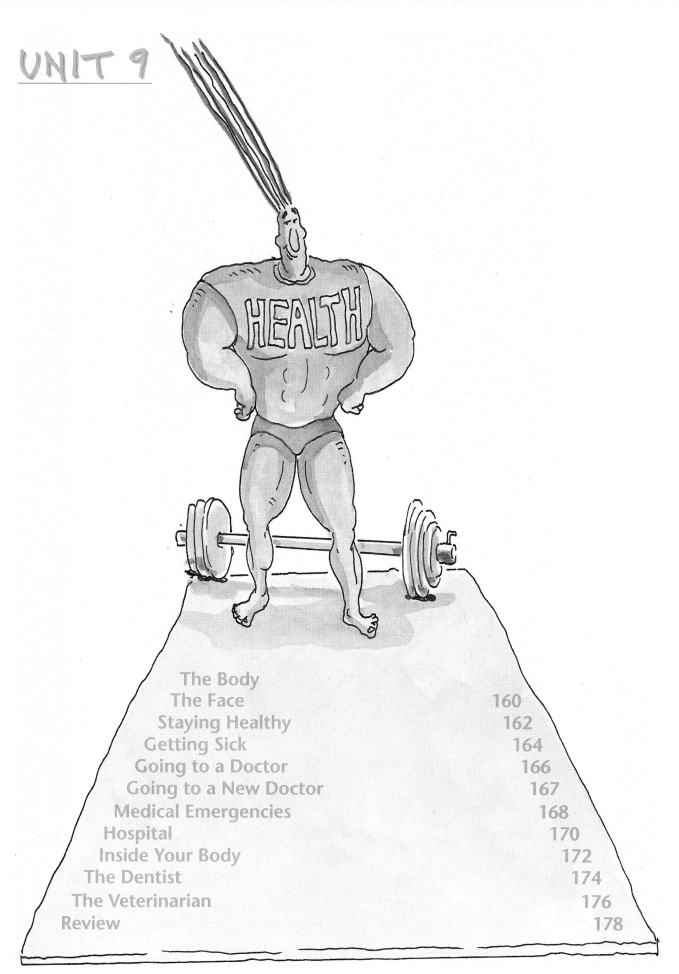

THE BODY

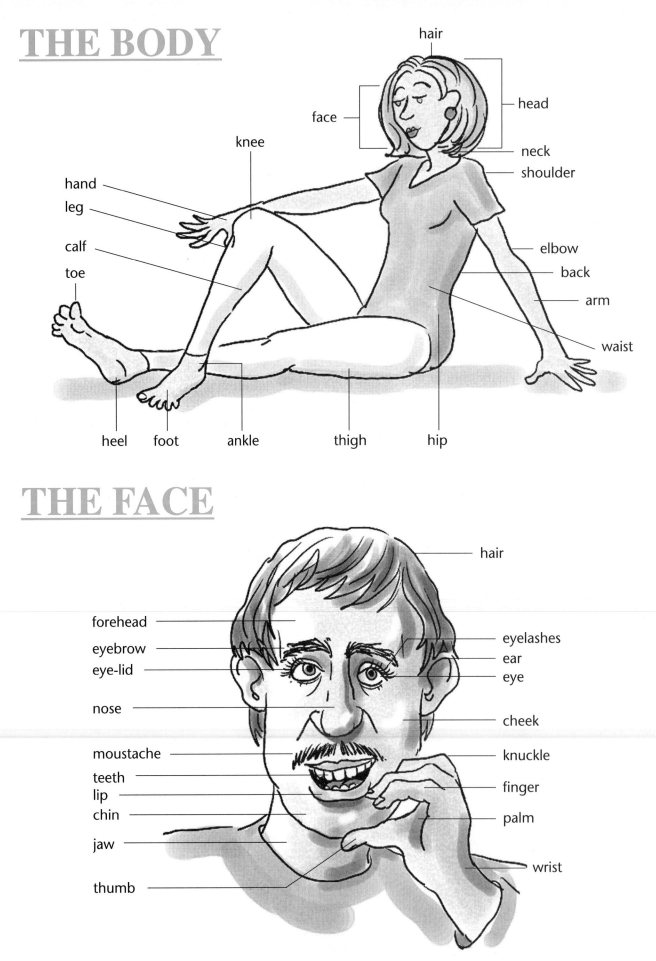

hair

head

face

neck

shoulder

knee

hand

leg

calf

toe

elbow

back

arm

waist

heel foot ankle thigh hip

THE FACE

hair

forehead

eyebrow

eye-lid

nose

moustache

teeth

lip

chin

jaw

thumb

eyelashes

ear

eye

cheek

knuckle

finger

palm

wrist

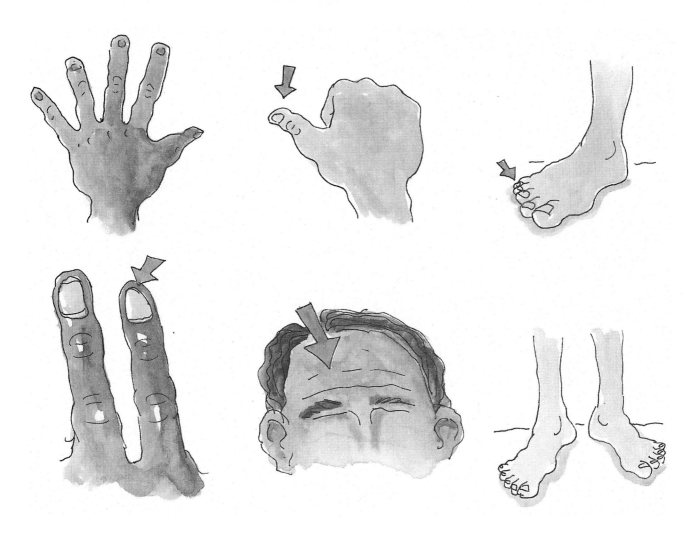

Group Game: *"What is it?"*

Work in groups of six. • *Choose a leader.*

> **Leader:** *Think about a part of the body.* • *Don't say what it is.*
>   **Group:** *Ask the leader YES/NO questions.*
> **Leader:** *Answer "Yes" or "No."*
>   **Group:** *Try to guess the word. Whoever guesses is the new leader.*

Class Game: *"Follow the Leader"*

Practise these instructions with your teacher. • *Close your book.* • *Listen to your teacher.* • *Follow the instructions.*

1. Stand up.
2. Nod your head ("yes").
3. Shake your head ("no").
4. Raise your left hand.
5. Touch your toes.
6. Put your hands on your hips.
7. Bend to the right.
8. Sit down.

STAYING HEALTHY

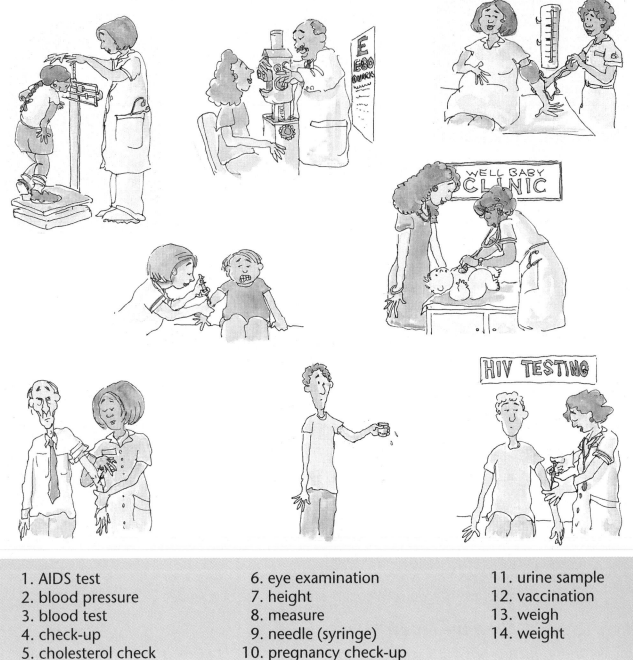

1. AIDS test	6. eye examination	11. urine sample
2. blood pressure	7. height	12. vaccination
3. blood test	8. measure	13. weigh
4. check-up	9. needle (syringe)	14. weight
5. cholesterol check	10. pregnancy check-up	

Look in the telephone directory for the hospital or walk-in clinic near your home.

What Are They Doing?

(Match the sentence with the corresponding picture!)

1. The nurse is taking blood for a blood test.

2. The doctor is listening to the baby's heart with a stethoscope.

3. The nurse is giving the child an immunization shot.

4. The doctor is weighing and measuring the girl.

5. The doctor is examining the woman's eyes.

Work in groups of five. • How can you stay healthy? • Everyone in the group should contribute one answer to each question. • Compare your answers with the rest of the class.

What is a nutritious meal?

	Student's name	Advice
1.		
2.		
3.		
4.		
5.		

What is the best kind of exercise ?

	Student's name	Advice
1.		
2.		
3.		
4.		
5.		

How many hours of sleep do you need each night?

	Student's name	Advice
1.		
2.		
3.		
4.		
5.		

GETTING SICK

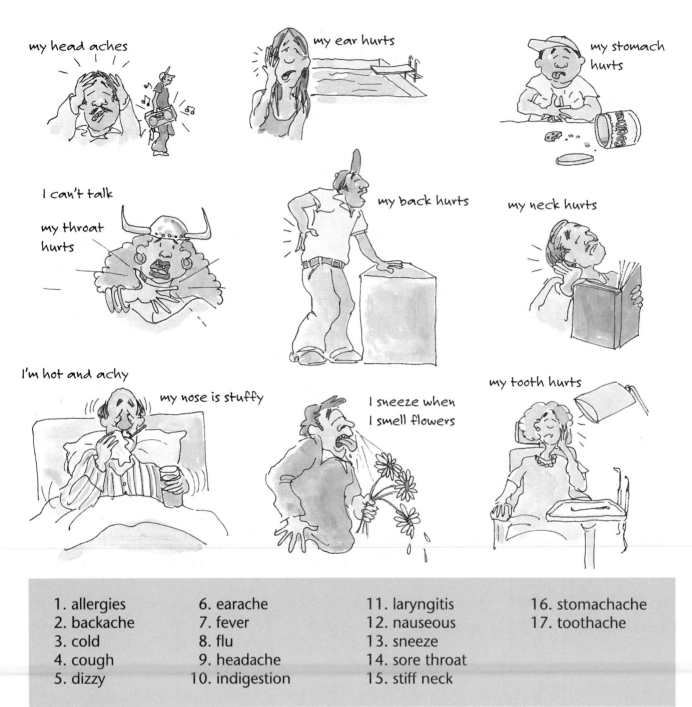

my head aches

my ear hurts

my stomach hurts

I can't talk

my throat hurts

my back hurts

my neck hurts

I'm hot and achy

my nose is stuffy

I sneeze when I smell flowers

my tooth hurts

1. allergies	6. earache	11. laryngitis	16. stomachache
2. backache	7. fever	12. nauseous	17. toothache
3. cold	8. flu	13. sneeze	
4. cough	9. headache	14. sore throat	
5. dizzy	10. indigestion	15. stiff neck	

Class Discussion

1. What's wrong with these people? (What are they saying — I have a _____)
   — I feel _____)
2. How do you treat these common problems?
3. When do you go to the doctor for these problems?

Cross-Cultural Exchange

How do people in your native country treat these problems?

Group Game: *"What's the matter?"*

Work in groups of four or five. • *Pantomime one of these problems for your group.* • *No speaking!* • *Whoever guesses takes the next turn.*

Partner Activity

Decide what medicines are in this cabinet. • *Fill in the labels.* • *On the empty bottles, write something from YOUR medicine cabinet.* • *Compare your answers with the class.*

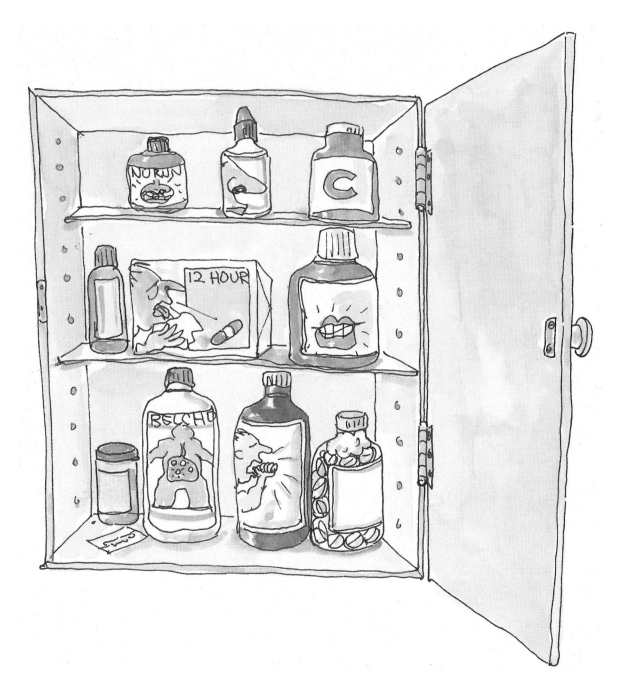

GOING TO A DOCTOR

> **ALLERGY**
> **ALLERGY & IMMUNOLOGY ASSOCIATES**
> **Arnold, Allan, M.D.**
>   326 North Ave., Weston 555-8070
> **Wykowski, Carla, M.D.**
>   4048 Wilson Dr., Yorkton 555-7890

> **CARDIOLOGY**
> **Cassidy, James A., M.D.**
>   57 Park Ave., Weston 555-7890
>   If No Answer Call...555-8382

> **DERMATOLOGY**
> **Natale, Ellen, M.D.**
>   2123 Main St., Albertville.......................555-3024

> **EAR, NOSE & THROAT**
> **Wu, Peter M., M.D.**
>   467 Valley View Dr., Weston..........................555-7974

> **FAMILY PRACTICE**
> **NEWTOWN FAMILY CARE ASSOCIATES**
>   230 Valley View Dr., Weston
>   New Patients Welcome
>   **Clinics** 555-0682
>   **Lindros, Ana, M.D.** 555-9188
>   **St. Clair, Paul, M.D.** 555-3025

> **GENERAL PRACTICE**
> **Henry, Richard, D.O.**
>   2441 River St., Yorkton 555-6017
> **Johnson, Margaret, M.D.**
> **General & Family Practice**
>   94 Wilson Dr., Yorkton 555-2198

> **INTERNAL MEDICINE**
> **Hossaini, Ali, M.D.**
> **Internal Medicine-Family Practice**
>   212 Main St., Weston.................................555-9744

> **NEUROLOGY**
> **UNIVERSITY PHYSICIANS' CENTRE**
> **Brigham, Peter, M.D.**
> **Papas, Irene, M.D.**
>   Toll Free....................................1-800-555-7654
>   501 Valley View Dr., Weston..........................555-2341

> **OBSTETRICS/GYNECOLOGY**
> **BIRTH AND WOMAN'S HEALTH CENTRE**
>   376 River St., Weston 555-7391

> **ONCOLOGY**
> **OLDTOWN CANCER CENTRE**
>   127 North Ave., Weston.................................555-6090
>   Cancer Helpline 1-800-555-HELP

> **OPHTHAMOLOGY**
> **VALLEY EYE & LASER**
> **Kaplan, Joan, M.D.**
> **Harris, John, M.D.**
>   350 Wilson Dr., Yorkton 555-2135

> **PEDIATRICS**
> **Rivers, Gloria, M.D.**
>   417 North Ave., Weston.................................555-3338

> **PSYCHIATRY**
> **Bassu, Sadru, M.D.**
>   Board Certified
>   438 Park Ave., Suite 6, Albertville...................555-5974

> **PULMONOLOGY**
> **Kehrberg, Martha, M.D.**
>   617 Valley View Dr., Weston..........................555-3019

> **RADIOLOGY**
> **Jorgensen, Eric, M.D.**
>   127 North Ave., Yorkton................................555-6090

Group Decision

Work in groups of five or six. • *Decide which doctor you need.* • *Report your decisions to the class.*

1. You have rash and your skin is itchy. _____

2. You get headaches when you read. _____

3. You think you are pregnant. _____

4. You sneeze a lot when you are outdoors. _____

5. Your baby has a fever and won't eat. _____

6. You need a medical check-up as a requirement for your health insurance. _____

7. You are depressed all the time. _____

8. You need a chest x-ray. _____

9. You have too many earaches. _____

10. You had a heart attack and need a check-up. _____

GOING TO A NEW DOCTOR

With Your Partner:

How do you find a doctor when you move to a new city?

The first time you go to a new doctor, you fill out a health history form. Fill this one out. Then role play visiting the doctor for a check-up. Ask the questions on this form.

PATIENT INFORMATION

NAME _____   DATE OF BIRTH _____

ADDRESS _____   AGE _____

POSTAL CODE_____   PHONE (_____) _____

EMPLOYER'S NAME

_____

EMPLOYER'S ADDRESS _____   POSTAL CODE _____

BUSINESS PHONE (_____) _____   SOCIAL INSURANCE NO. _____

NEAREST OF KIN _____   PHONE (_____) _____

ADDRESS _____   POSTAL CODE _____

DRUG ALLERGIES ❑ YES ❑ NO   IF YES, LIST _____

REFERRING PHYSICIAN: _____

INSURANCE COV.	IDENT. NO.	COV. CODE NO.	SUBSCRIBER'S NAME
HEALTH CARD	_____	_____	_____
BLUE CROSS	_____	_____	_____

AUTO ACCIDENT   DATE OF ACCIDENT _____   DATE OF DISABILITY_____

COMPENSATION   DATE OF ACCIDENT _____   DATE OF DISABILITY_____

OTHER: _____

_____

_____

_____

_____

_____

MEDICAL EMERGENCIES

1. accident	7. cut	13. ointment	19. stroke
2. bandage	8. EKG (electrocardiagram)	14. oxygen	20. wash
3. bleed	9. emergency room	15. poison	21. x-ray
4. burn	10. fall	16. pulse	
5. cast	11. heart attack	17. stitches	
6. concussion	12. ice pack	18. stomach pump	

Class Discussion

Tell the stories together as a class. • What would you do in these situations? • Who has had a medical emergency? • Tell the class what happened.

Partner Activity

Decide what to do in these emergencies. • Report your answers to the class.

1. If someone next to you in the bus faints, what do you do?
2. If a person falls down a flight of stairs, what do you do?
3. If you cut yourself badly with a knife, what do you do?
4. If you step on a rusty nail, what do you do?
5. If you accidentally take poison, what do you do?

Group Decision

Work in groups of five. • Decide what supplies to use for each of the following emergencies.
• Report your decisions to the class.

bee sting	broken arm	splinter
sprained ankle	gash	sliver

Community Activity

Answer these questions with your class. • Find out the missing information and report to the class.

1. What is the name of the closest hospital in your neighbourhood?
2. Does the hospital have an emergency room? Where is it?
3. Did you ever go to the emergency room? Why?
4. Does your insurance cover emergency room visits?
5. What number do you call for emergencies?

HOSPITAL

1. blood transfusion	7. intensive care unit (ICU)	13. semi-private
2. broken leg	8. intravenous (IV)	14. unconscious
3. coma	9. nurse's station	15. visiting hours
4. get well card	10. orderly	16. visitor
5. hospital bed	11. patient	
6. information desk	12. private	

What's the Story?

Work in groups of five. • Write a story about the hospital scene. • Everyone in the group should contribute at least two sentences. • Read your story to the class.

1. Who are the people in this picture?
2. Who is sick? What is wrong?
3. What is the nurse doing?
4. What is the patient in room 208 doing? in room 209?
5. Who are the visitors? What room are they going to visit?

Hospital Signs

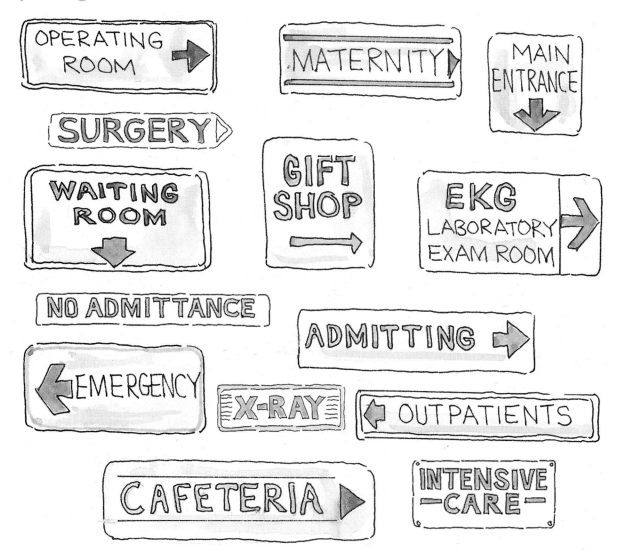

Partner Activity

Partner's name _____

Decide which sign to follow. • *Report your answers to the class.*

1. You want to buy a gift for your friend. _____
2. You are hungry and want to get some lunch after your visit. _____
3. You need to get a chest x-ray. _____
4. Your sister is having a baby and you need a place to wait. _____
5. You have to have a blood test. _____
6. Your father is having chest pains. _____

INSIDE YOUR BODY

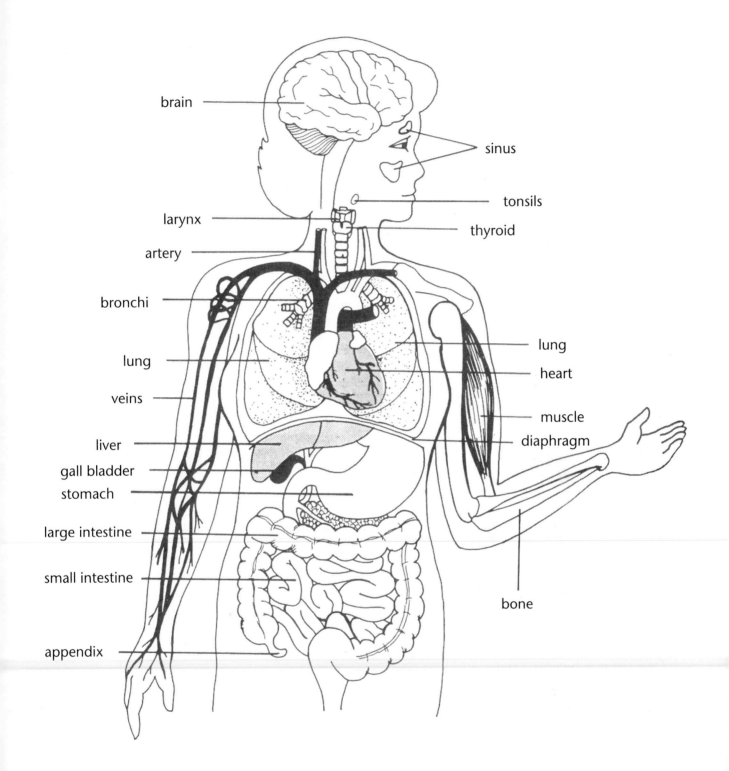

brain

sinus

tonsils

larynx

thyroid

artery

bronchi

lung

lung

heart

veins

muscle

liver

diaphragm

gall bladder

stomach

large intestine

small intestine

bone

appendix

Group Activity

Work in groups of five or six. • *Decide on the part of the body where the problem is.* • *Compare your answers with the class.*

MEDICAL PROBLEM	PART OF THE BODY
1. heart attack	heart _____
2. tonsillitis	_____
3. lung cancer	_____
4. kidney infection	_____
5. gall stones	_____
6. appendicitis	_____
7. broken arm	_____
8. stroke	_____
9. tuberculosis	_____
10. other _____	_____

Cross-Cultural Exchange

Compare the treatments for these problems in different countries. • *Which treatments do you prefer?*

Group Game: *"Gossip!"*

Work in groups of eight. • *Choose a leader.* • *Close your books.* • *What are the people saying?*

Leader: (To the first student) Read the secret on page 226. Close your book. Whisper the secret to the student sitting next to you.

That Student: Whisper the secret to the student sitting next to you, etc.

Last Student: Write the secret on the board or tell the class.

Class: Check the secret on page 226. Which group had the most accurate secret?

THE DENTIST

Vocabulary Activity: What a Dentist Does

Read this with your class. Discuss the vocabulary and fill in the captions below.

A dentist cleans teeth, takes x-rays of teeth, fills cavities, and treats gum diseases. An oral surgeon extracts teeth and does other oral surgery. An orthodontist puts braces on teeth. A dental assistant helps the dentist.

1. abscess	4. cavity	7. dentist	10. gums
2. anesthetic	5. cleaning	8. dentist's chair	11. receptionist
3. braces	6. dental hygienist	9. extraction	12. waiting room

Partners' Interview: Your Teeth

Ask your partner these questions. Report your interview to the class.

1. Have you ever had a toothache? What did you do about it?

2. Have you ever had your teeth cleaned at a dentist's office? How often? Do people in your native country have their teeth cleaned regularly?

3. Have you had any fillings? Did the drilling hurt? Do you prefer to have Novocain when you have a tooth filled?

4. Did you ever have a tooth extracted? Was it a wisdom tooth? Did you have Novocain? Gas? Sodium Pentothal?

5. Are there any differences between dental care in your native country and in Canada? Do people in your native country ever have gold fillings or gold caps put on their teeth?

6. How do you feel about going to the dentist? Do you ever avoid it?

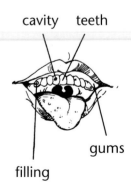

cavity   teeth

gums

filling

Partner Role Play

You have a toothache and can't eat. • *Make a "telephone call" for an appointment with the dentist.* • *Present your conversation to the class.*

What's the Story?

Work in groups of five. • *Choose one of the patients and write a story for him or her.* • *Everyone in the group should contribute at least two sentences.* • *Read your story to the class.* • *Answer these questions:*

1. What is the patient's name?
2. How old is she/he?
3. Why is this patient at the dentist's office?
4. How does she/he feel? Why?
5. How often does she/he visit the dentist?
6. Will she/he have an anesthetic?
7. What will the dentist (or the hygienist) do?
8. Does she/he like the dentist? Why or why not?
9. How will the patient feel when she/he leaves the office?
10. Where will she/he go?

Cross-Cultural Exchange

In some cultures, the "Tooth Fairy" takes children's baby teeth from under their pillows and leaves money. • *Is there a special custom in your native country for baby teeth?* • *Tell the class.*

THE VETERINARIAN

1. assistant	5. examining table	9. rabies tag
2. board	6. inoculation	10. veterinarian
3. cage	7. leash	
4. carrying case	8. licence	

What's the Story?

Work in groups of five or six. • Pick a pet in the picture. • Write a story. • Everyone in the group should contribute at least one sentence. • Read your story to the class. • Answer these questions:

1. What is the pet's name?
2. How old is it?
3. Why is the pet at the vet's?
4. What will the owner tell the vet?
5. What will the vet tell the owner?
6. What will the owner and the pet do after the visit?

Class Discussion

1. Do you have a pet? What kind?
2. What is your pet's name?
3. What kind of pet did you have as a child?
4. What kind of pet would you like to have? Why?
6. In your country, do people like to have pets? What are the most popular pets in your country?
7. What are some names for pets in your country?
8. Why do people take their pets to the vet?
9. Who is the best vet in your neighbourhood?

Group Problem Posing/Problem Solving

Work in groups of three or four. • *Choose a situation.* • *State the problem.* • *Find a solution.* • *Report your decision to the class.*

Speech

Tell the class about pets in your country. • *Use these questions as a guide.*

1. Do many people have pets?
2. What are the most popular pets?
3. What are popular names for pets?

REVIEW

Write

Fill in this crossword puzzle. • *Check your answers with your partner.*

ACROSS

10.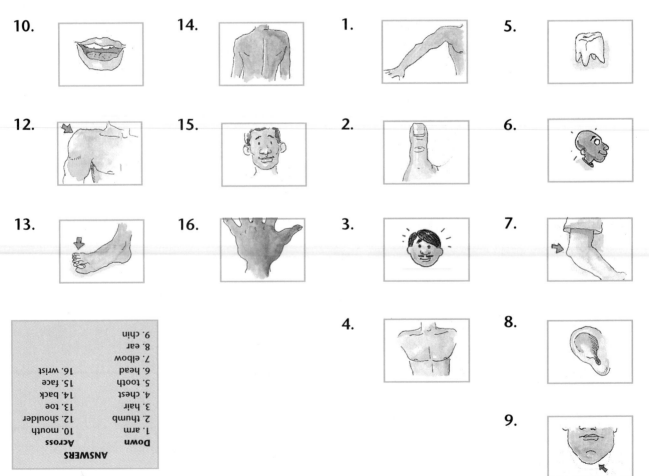
14.
12.
15.
13.
16.

DOWN

1.
5.
2.
6.
3.
7.
4.
8.
9.

UNIT 10

LEISURE

LEISURE TIME

1. go camping	6. go to the movies	11. play with a pet
2. go for a walk	7. jog	12. read a book
3. go swimming	8. play dominoes	13. take photographs
4. go to a baseball game	9. play soccer	14. travel
5. go to a party	10. play the guitar	15. watch TV

Group Vocabulary Challenge

Work in groups of five or six. • *Make a list of leisure time activities.* • *Read your list to the class.*
• *The group with the most activities is the winner!*

Group Survey

Ask everyone in your group these questions. • *Check SOMETIMES or NEVER.* • *Count the answers.* • *Report your group's results to the class.* • *Write the class' results on the board.*

In your leisure time, do you:	SOMETIMES	NEVER
1. watch TV?	_____	_____
2. go to the movies?	_____	_____
3. read?	_____	_____
4. play with a pet?	_____	_____
5. listen to music?	_____	_____
6. play a musical instrument?	_____	_____
7. watch sports?	_____	_____
8. play a sport?	_____	_____
9. travel?	_____	_____
10. go camping?	_____	_____
11. go to school?	_____	_____

Partner Interview

Partner 's name _____

Practise these questions with your teacher. • *Then ask your partner.*

1. When do you have leisure time?
2. What do you like to do most in your leisure time?
3. What do you like to do on a rainy day?
4. What do you like to do in the summer?
5. What will you do on your next holiday?

What's the Story?

Work in groups of five. • *Write a story for the picture.* • *Everyone in the group should contribute at least one sentence.* • *Read your story to the class.*

GOING OUT

1. amusement park	5. dance	9. host	13. painting
2. club	6. dressed up	10. museum	14. roller coaster
3. concert	7. friend	11. musician	15. sculpture
4. cotton candy	8. guest	12. opera	16. singer

Class Discussion

What is happening in these pictures? • Discuss each one.

Find Someone Who

What do you like to do when you go out? • *Review the vocabulary with your teacher.* • *Fill in the name of someone who . . .*

1. _____ likes to ride a roller coaster.
2. _____ goes to church every week.
3. _____ likes to visit museums.
4. _____ likes to go to parties.
5. _____ likes to go dancing.
6. _____ likes to go to concerts.
7. _____ goes out with friends every day.
8. _____ has gone to an opera.
9. _____ likes to go to the movies.
10. _____ likes to stay home.

Partner Role Play   Partner's Name _____

Write a telephone conversation. • *One partner invites the other to do something.* • *Present your conversation to the class.*

Community Activity

Bring a local newspaper to class. • *Look in the ENTERTAINMENT section.* • *Are there any interesting events?* • *How much do they cost?* • *What day and time do they begin?* • *Plan a class field trip.* • *Enjoy!*

WATCHING TELEVISION

1. cable	4. comedy	8. mystery	12. talk show
2. cartoons	5. commercial	9. program	13. variety show
3. channel	6. game show	10. sad	
	7. late night show	11. soap opera	

Find Someone Who

Read this exercise with your teacher. Then find someone in your class who:

1. watches the news on TV _____
2. watches sports on TV _____
3. watches movies on TV _____
4. likes situation comedies _____
5. likes soap operas _____
6. likes game shows _____
7. doesn't like to watch TV _____
8. watches weather reports on TV _____
9. doesn't like any TV commercials _____
10. watches TV late at night _____

Group Decision

Work in groups of five. • The people in this picture are looking for a video to watch together tonight. • What kind of video does each person prefer? • What kind of video will they enjoy together? • Report your decision to the class.

Partner Interview

Partner's name _____

Practise these questions with your teacher. • Then ask your partner.

1. Do you ever rent videos?
2. Where is the best place to rent videos in your neighbourhood?
3. What kind of videos do you like?
4. What kind of TV programs do you like?
5. Do you ever watch late night TV?
6. Which do you like better: to watch TV or to watch videos? Why?

Community Activity

Use a real TV schedule from the newspaper. • Choose one day of the week. • Decide which programs to watch for that day. • Write the name, channel, and time of each program. • Report your decision to the class.

MOVIES

1. actor	4. audience	7. refreshment stand	10. usher
2. actress	5. candy	8. screen	11. video game
3. aisle	6. popcorn	9. ticket	

Class Discussion

1. What was the last movie you saw?
2. What movies are in the theatres now?
3. What new movie do you want to see?
4. What do you like to eat and drink at the movies?
5. Do you like to play video games in the movie lobby?
6. How much does an admission ticket cost?

Community Activity

1. Select a movie from the movie page. What time is it playing? Where is it playing?
2. Discuss the ratings of movies: What do they mean?

Conversation Squares

First write your own answers. • *Then ask your partners the questions.* • *Write their answers.* • *Compare your group answers with other groups.* • *How many students have the same favourites?*

Favourite	You:_____	Partner 1:_____	Partner 2:_____
1. Movie	_____	_____	_____
2. Actress	_____	_____	_____
3. Actor	_____	_____	_____
4. Comedian	_____	_____	_____

INDIVIDUAL SPORTS

1. aerobics	5. golf	9. running	13. tennis
2. bicycling	6. gymnastics	10. skating	14. working out
3. bowling	7. hiking	11. skiing	15. wrestling
4. boxing	8. jogging	12. swimming	16. yoga

Group Survey

Ask everyone in your group these questions. • Write all the answers. • Compare your group's opinions with the rest of the class.

1. Which is the most difficult sport? _____
2. Which is the easiest? _____
3. Which is the most exciting? _____
4. Which is the most dangerous? _____
5. Which is the most fun to watch on TV? _____
6. Which of these sports is exercise? _____

Class Game: *"What is your favourite way to exercise?"*

Think. • Write. • Fold your paper. • Make a pile of papers. • Open one. • Ask "What am I doing?" • Have the class guess the exercise.

Community Activity

Where can you play a sport? • Use the telephone directory. • Find out this information:

Is there a:	YES	NO	WHERE?
1. skating rink?	_____	_____	_____
2. bowling alley?	_____	_____	_____
3. swimming pool?	_____	_____	_____
4. tennis court?	_____	_____	_____
5. golf course?	_____	_____	_____
6. ski area?	_____	_____	_____
7. bicycle trail?	_____	_____	_____

TEAM SPORTS

1. base	7. down	13. goal	19. net	25. shoot
2. baseball	8. dribble	14. goal post	20. out	26. soccer
3. basket	9. field hockey	15. hit	21. pass	27. tackle
4. basketball	10. football	16. hockey	22. pitch	28. touchdown
5. catch	11. foul	17. hoop	23. referee	29. umpire
6. coach	12. free throw	18. kick	24. run	

Group Discussion

Work in groups of eight. • *Discuss these questions.* • *Report your answers to the class.*

1. Did you ever play on a team? Which one(s)?
2. When did you play?
3. Where did you play?
4. What position did you play?
5. Do you like to watch team sports on TV? What do you like to watch?
6. Do you ever go to a sports event? Which ones do you like to attend?
7. Do you have a favourite team? Which one?

Conversation Squares

First write your answers. • *Then ask your partners the questions.* • *Write their answers.* • *Compare your group answers with other groups.* • *How many students have the same favourites?*

Favourite	You:_____	Partner 1:_____	Partner 2:_____
Sport	_____	_____	_____
Team	_____	_____	_____
Player	_____	_____	_____

Community Activity

What sport season is it now? • *Which teams are winning?* • *Choose a game to watch on TV and report to the class.* • *Who played?* • *Who won?* • *What was the score?* • *What interesting things happened?*

Cross-Cultural Exchange

What is the most popular team sport in your country? • *Who is the most popular sports hero in your country?*

AT THE PARK

Find Someone Who

Review the vocabulary with your teacher. • *Fill in the name of someone who. . .*

1. _____ likes to jog in the park.
2. _____ likes to feed the birds in the park.
3. _____ likes to feed the squirrels in the park.
4. _____ likes to take children to the playground.
5. _____ likes to fly a kite.

Strip Story

Work in groups of four. • *Look at the pictures.* • *Decide what is happening.* • *Tell the story to the class.*

Cross-Cultural Exchange

What do parks look like in your hometown? • *When do people go to the park?* • *What do they do in there?* • *What is the name of a famous park in your country?* • *Describe it to the class.* • *Can you name a popular park in your city?* • *Do you go there often?*

TAKING A TRIP

1. by airplane	5. luggage/baggage	9. suitcase	13. travel brochure
2. by bus	6. on a cruise ship	10. ticket	14. trip
3. by train	7. passport	11. tour	
4. camera	8. sightseeing	12. travel agent	

What's the Story?

Work in groups of three. • Write a story about this picture. • Everyone in the group should contribute at least one sentence. • Read your story to the class.

Group Vocabulary Challenge

Work in groups of three or four. • What would you pack for a trip to a tropical island? • Make a list. • Read your group's list to the class. • Make a list of all vocabulary on the board. • The group with the longest list is the winner!

194

Group Discussion

Work in groups of five. • *Discuss these questions.* • *Report the answers to the class.*

1. What do you like to do on vacation?
2. How do you prefer to travel?
3. Do you visit your family on vacation? Where do they live?
4. Do you ever travel to another country? Where do you go?
5. What is the most beautiful place you have ever been to?

Write

Imagine you are on vacation. • *Complete the postcard.* • *Address it to your English class.* • *Read it to your class.*

Hi.

Having a wonderful time in _____. I'm enjoying the _____. The weather is _____.

_____.

Place stamp here

Cross-Cultural Exchange

What is the best place to visit in your country? • *Tell the class about it.* • *Do you have a postcard or photo of a special place in your country?* • *Bring the card or photo to class.* • *Tell the class about the place.* • *Make a bulletin board with everyone's postcards.*

AT THE BEACH

1. beach	6. life preserver	11. sand castle	16. suntan
2. beach towel	7. pail	12. shovel	17. surf
3. beach umbrella	8. rescuing	13. speedboat	18. surfboard
4. drowning	9. sailboat	14. sunbathing	19. water skiing
5. lifeguard	10. sand	15. sunburn	

What's the Story?

Decide who you would like to be in this picture. • *Write a story.* • *Read your story to the class.*

CAMPING

1. backpack
2. bear
3. campfire
4. deer
5. fishing
6. fox
7. hiking
8. lantern
9. mosquito
10. mountain climbing
11. porcupine
12. quills
13. raccoon
14. set up camp
15. skunk
16. sleeping bag
17. snake
18. sunrise
19. swimming
20. tent
21. trailer
22. wild animal

Do people in your native country go camping? • *Where do they go?* • *Is camping the same or different in Canada?* • *Send for camping information from your province or from a place you want to visit.* • *Consult a camping atlas for sites near your destination.* • *What facilities does the site have?*

THE LIBRARY

1. author
2. card catalogue
3. check out
4. circulation desk
5. dictionary
6. due
7. encyclopedia
8. late fine
9. librarian
10. library card
11. magazine
12. overdue
13. periodicals
14. reference
15. stacks (shelves)
16. subject
17. title

Partner Vocabulary Challenge

Partner's name _____

Make a list of all the people in the library and what they are doing. • *Compare your list with another pair.*

Community Activity

With your class, plan a visit to the library in your school or your community. • *Make a list of some questions to ask.*

SCHOOL

Class Discussion

1. What other courses can you take where you study English?
2. Have you ever taken another course? Which one? When is it offered?
3. Would you like to take another course? What course?
4. Do many adults go to school in your country? What kinds of courses can adults take?

Group Game: *Gossip!*

Work in groups of eight. • Choose a leader. • Close your books. • What are the people saying?

Leader:	*Read the secret on page 226. Close your book. Whisper the secret to the student sitting next to you.*
That Student:	*Whisper the secret to the student sitting next to you, etc.*
Last Student:	*Write the secret on the board or tell the class.*
Class:	*Check the secret on page 226. Which group had the most accurate secret?*

Community Activity

Get a catalogue from an adult school. • Pick out courses you would like to take. • How much English is required? • What did most of the students in the class choose? • Sign up and enjoy!!

REVIEW

Partner's name _____

Practise these questions with your teacher. • *Then ask your partner.*

1. What is today's date?
2. What is your name?
3. What do you like to do in your leisure time?
4. Where do you prefer to spend your time?
5. How often do you watch TV?
6. What do you watch on TV?
7. What is your favourite physical exercise?
8. What would you like to try someday?
9. What do you never want to do?
10. Where would you like to visit someday?

Write

Write about your partner in your journal.

Write about your partner in your journal.

Journal

_____
(1)

My partner's name is _____. When he/she
(2)

has leisure time, he/she likes to _____. He/she
(3)

prefers to spend time _____. He/she watches
(4)

TV _____. When he/she watches TV, he/she prefers
(5)

to watch _____.
(6)

His/her favourite physical exercise is _____. He/She
(7)

would like to try _____ someday, but he/she never
(8)

wants to try _____. He/She would like to visit _____
(9)   (10)

someday.

Tell the Class

Read your journal to the class. • *Tell the class about your partner.*

Cross-Cultural Exchange

Bring in some typical music from your native country. • *Tell the class about the music.* •
Is there a special dance for the music? • *Teach it to the class.*

200

EVALUATION

Writing Activity: Course Evaluation

At the end of many courses for adults in Canada, the teacher asks the students to evaluate the course and make suggestions for the future. • *Answer these questions for your teacher.* • *Try to answer honestly.* • *Your answers will help your teacher to plan for the next term.*

1. What was the best thing about this course?
2. What do you think your teacher should do the same way next term?
3. What do you think your teacher should change next term?
4. Do you think there should be more homework? less homework? the same homework?
5. Do you think there should be more tests? fewer tests? the same number of tests?

With Your Group: Self-Evaluation

In some courses, teachers ask students to evaluate their own learning. • *Answer these questions for yourself.* • *Share your answers with your group and your teacher.*

1. What did you learn in this course?
2. Do you feel good about your effort in this course? If you could take the course again, would you study more? less? the same amount? the same way?
3. How do you feel about your English now? What do you need to work on?

APPENDIX

PRINTING UPPER-CASE LETTERS (CAPITAL LETTERS)

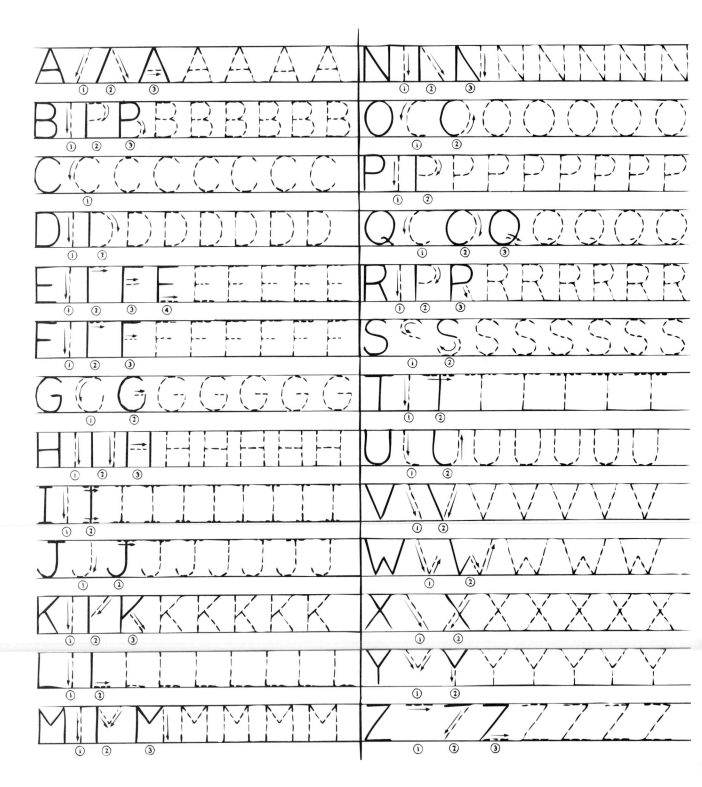

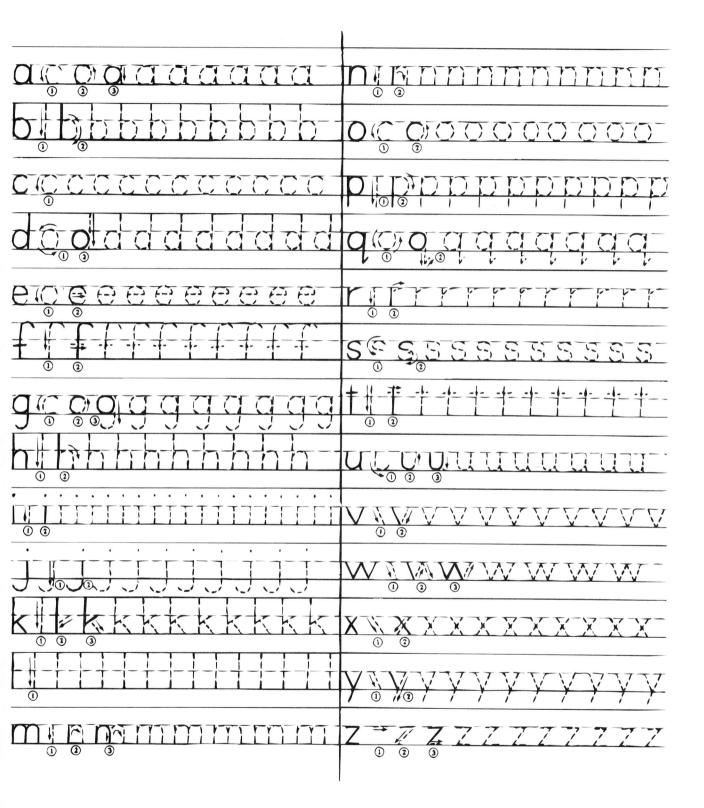

WRITING UPPER-CASE LETTERS (CAPITAL LETTERS)

WRITING LOWER-CASE LETTERS
(SMALL LETTERS)

Writing Book: English in Everyday Life, Tina Kasloff Carver, Sandra Douglas Fotinos, and Christie Kay Olson. Copyright © 1982. Reprinted by permission of Prentice-Hall, Inc.

NUMBERS

Cardinal Numbers

1	one	26	twenty-six
2	two	27	twenty-seven
3	three	28	twenty-eight
4	four	29	twenty-nine
5	five	30	thirty
6	six	40	forty
7	seven	50	fifty
8	eight	60	sixty
9	nine	70	seventy
10	ten	80	eighty
11	eleven	90	ninety
12	twelve	100	one hundred
13	thirteen	200	two hundred
14	fourteen	300	three hundred
15	fifteen	400	four hundred
16	sixteen	500	five hundred
17	seventeen	600	six hundred
18	eighteen	700	seven hundred
19	nineteen	800	eight hundred
20	twenty	900	nine hundred
21	twenty-one	1,000	one thousand
22	twenty-two	10,000	ten thousand
23	twenty-three	100,000	one hundred thousand
24	twenty-four	1,000,000	one million
25	twenty-five		

Ordinal Numbers

first (1st)	twenty-sixth (26th)
second (2nd)	twenty-seventh (27th)
third (3rd)	twenty-eighth (28th)
fourth (4th)	twenty-ninth (29th)
fifth (5th)	thirtieth (30th)
sixth (6th)	fortieth (40th)
seventh (7th)	fiftieth (50th)
eighth (8th)	sixtieth (60th)
ninth (9th)	seventieth (70th)
tenth (10th)	eightieth (80th)
eleventh (11th)	ninetieth (90th)
twelfth (12th)	one hundredth (100th)
thirteenth (13th)	one thousandth
fourteenth (14th)	one millionth
fifteenth (15th)	
sixteenth (16th)	
seventeenth (17th)	
eighteenth (18th)	
nineteenth (19th)	
twentieth (20th)	
twenty-first (21st)	
twenty-second (22nd)	
twenty-third (23rd)	
twenty-fourth (24th)	
twenty-fifth (25th)	

MEASURES AND EQUIVALENTS

1. metres to yards, multiply the number of metres by 1.09.

2. yards to metres, multiply the number of yards by .91.

3. metres to inches, multiply the number of metres by 39.37.

4. inches to metres, multiply the number of inches by .0254.

5. millimetres to inches, multiply the number of millimetres by .04.

6. inches to millimetres, multiply the number of inches by 25.4.

7. kilometres to miles, multiply the number of kilometres by .62.

8. miles to kilometres, multiply the number of miles by 1.61.

9. litres to liquid quarts, multiply the number of litres by 1.06.

10. liquid quarts to litres, multiply the number of liquid quarts by 95.

11. litres to dry quarts, multiply the number of litres by .91.

12. dry quarts to litres, multiply the number of dry quarts by 1.1.

13. kilograms to pounds, multiply the number of kilograms by 2.2.

14. pounds to kilograms, multiply the number of pounds by .45.

15. centimetres to inches, multiply the number of centimetres by .4.

16. inches to centimetres, multiply the number of inches by 2.54.

Measure of Length

Metric to Imperial units:

1 metre = 39.37 inches
    = 3.28 feet
    = 1.09 yards
1 centimetre = .4 inch
1 millimetre = .04 inch
1 kilometre = .62 mile

Imperial to metric units:

1 inch = 25.4 millimetres
    = 2.54 centimetres
    = 0.254 metre
1 foot = .3 metre
1 yard = .91 metre
1 mile = 1.61 kilometres

Measure of Capacity—liquid measure

Metric to Imperial units:

1 litre = 1.06 liquid quarts

Imperial to metric units:

1 liquid quart = .95 litre

Measure of Capacity—dry measure

Metric to Imperial units:

1 litre = .91 dry quart

Imperial to metric units:

1 dry quart = 1.1 litres

Measure of Weight

Metric to Imperial units:

1 gram = .04 ounce
1 kilogram = 2.2 pounds
1 metric ton = 2204.62 pounds

Imperial to metric units:

1 ounce = 28.35 grams
1 pound = .45 kilogram
1 short ton = .91 metric ton

Measure of Area

Metric to Imperial units:

1 square centimetre = .16 square inches
1 square metre = 10.76 square feet
    = 1.2 square yards
1 square kilometre = .39 square miles

Imperial to metric units:

1 square inch = 6.45 square centimetres
1 square foot = .09 square metre
1 square yard = .84 square metre
1 square mile = 2.59 square kilometres

Measure of Volume

Metric to Imperial units:

1 cubic centimetre = .06 cubic inch
1 cubic metre = 35.31 cubic feet
1 cubic metre = 1.31 cubic yards
1 litre = .04 cubic foot

Imperial to metric units:
1 cubic inch = 16.39 cubic centimetres
1 cubic foot = .03 cubic metre
1 cubic yard = .76 cubic metre

Imperial Measures

weight
ounce (oz.)
  16 oz. = 1 lb.
pound (lb.)

length
inch (in. or ")
  12" = 1'
foot (ft. or ')
  3 ' = 1 yd.
yard (yd.)
  1760 yds. = 1 mi.
mile (mi.)

liquid
pint (pt.)
  2 pts. = 1 qt.
quart (qt.)
  4 qts. = 1 gal.
gallon (gal.)

PROVINCIAL HOLIDAYS

New Year's Day	— January 1
Good Friday	— The Friday before Easter
Easter Monday	— The Monday following Easter
Victoria Day	— The Monday before May 24th
St. Jean Baptiste Day	— June 24th (Quebec only)
Canada Day	— July 1st (all provinces except Newfoundland)
	— Memorial Day (Newfoundland)
Civic Holiday	— Observed the first Monday in August under various names:
	— British Columbia Day (British Columbia)
	— Heritage Day (Alberta)
	— Saskatchewan Day (Saskatchewan)
	— Civic Holiday (Manitoba)
	— Simcoe Day (Ontario)
	— New Brunswick Day (New Brunswick)
	— Civic Holiday (Northwest Territories)
Discovery Day	— 3rd Monday in August (Yukon Territory)
Labour Day	— The first Monday in September
Thanksgiving Day	— The second Monday in October
Remembrance Day	— November 11th
Christmas Day	— December 25th
Boxing Day	— December 26th

PROVINCIAL NAMES, ABBREVIATIONS, AND CAPITAL CITIES OF CANADA

COUNTRY	CAPITAL
Canada	Ottawa

PROVINCE	CAPITAL
British Columbia (BC)	Victoria
Alberta (AB)	Edmonton
Saskatchewan (SK)	Regina
Manitoba (MB)	Winnipeg
Ontario (ON)	Toronto
Quebec (PQ)	Quebec City
New Brunswick (NB)	Fredericton
Nova Scotia (NS)	Halifax
Prince Edward Island (PE)	Charlottetown
Newfoundland (NF)	St. John's

Territory	Capital
Yukon Territory (YT)	White Horse
Northwest Territories (NT)	Yellowknife

CANADA

UNITED STATES OF AMERICA

Washington
Montana
North Dakota
Minnesota
New Hampshire
Vermont
Maine

Oregon
Idaho
South Dakota
Wisconsin
Michigan
Massachusetts

Wyoming
New York
Rhode Island
Connecticut

Nevada
Utah
Nebraska
Iowa
Pennsylvania
New Jersey
District of Columbia
Delaware
Maryland

Colorado
Illinois
Indiana
Ohio
West
Virginia
Virginia

California
Kansas
Missouri
Kentucky
North
Carolina

Arizona
New Mexico
Oklahoma
Arkansas
Tennessee
South
Carolina

Texas
Alabama
Georgia

Mississippi
Louisiana

Florida

Kilometres
0   320   640

Alaska

Hawaii

Kilometres
0   320 640

Kilometres
0   160 320

THE MIDDLE EAST

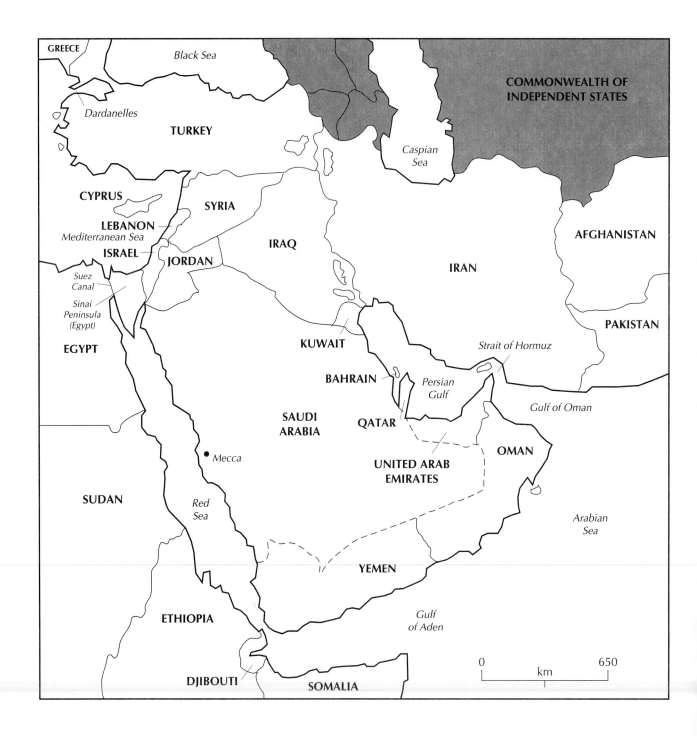

GREECE

Black Sea

Dardanelles

TURKEY

COMMONWEALTH OF
INDEPENDENT STATES

Caspian
Sea

CYPRUS

SYRIA

LEBANON

Mediterranean Sea

ISRAEL

JORDAN

IRAQ

AFGHANISTAN

IRAN

Suez
Canal

Sinai
Peninsula
(Egypt)

EGYPT

KUWAIT

PAKISTAN

Strait of Hormuz

BAHRAIN

Persian
Gulf

Gulf of Oman

SAUDI
ARABIA

QATAR

UNITED ARAB
EMIRATES

OMAN

• Mecca

SUDAN

Red
Sea

Arabian
Sea

YEMEN

ETHIOPIA

Gulf
of Aden

0   650
km

DJIBOUTI

SOMALIA

EUROPE

YUGOSLAVIA

Present Yugoslav Republics

1. MONTENEGRO
2. SERBIA

Former Yugoslav Republics

3. MACEDONIA
4. BOSNIA–
   HERCEGOVINA
5. CROATIA
6. SLOVENIA

SOUTHEAST ASIA

CENTRAL AND SOUTH AMERICA

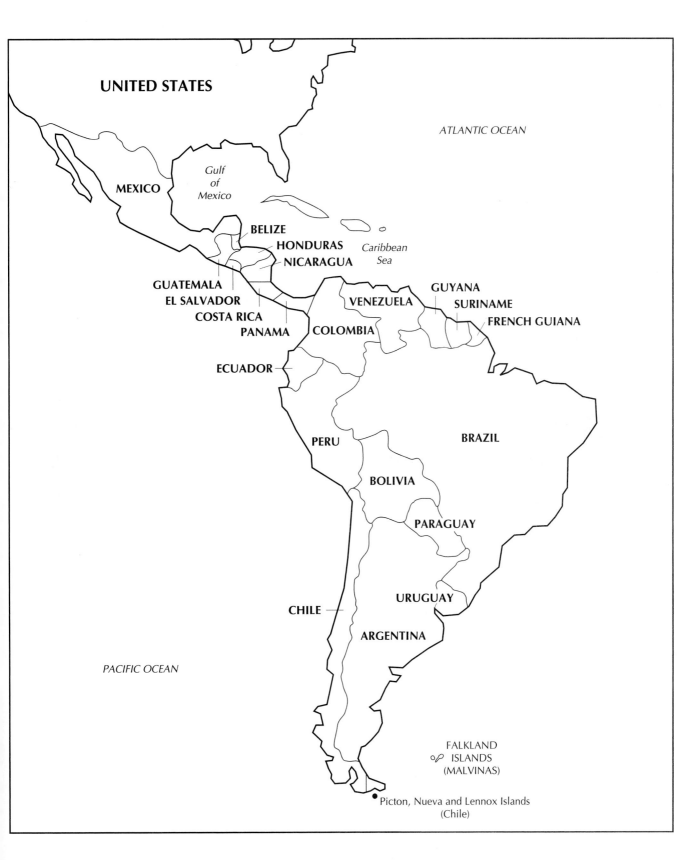

UNITED STATES

ATLANTIC OCEAN

MEXICO

*Gulf
of
Mexico*

BELIZE

HONDURAS

*Caribbean
Sea*

NICARAGUA

GUATEMALA

EL SALVADOR

COSTA RICA

PANAMA

VENEZUELA

COLOMBIA

GUYANA

SURINAME

FRENCH GUIANA

ECUADOR

PERU

BRAZIL

BOLIVIA

PARAGUAY

URUGUAY

CHILE

ARGENTINA

PACIFIC OCEAN

FALKLAND
ISLANDS
(MALVINAS)

Picton, Nueva and Lennox Islands
(Chile)

CANADA'S NATIONAL ANTHEM

O Canada!
    Our home and native land!
True patriot love
    in all thy sons command.
With glowing hearts
    we see thee rise,
The True North
    strong and free!
From far and wide,
    O Canada,
We stand on guard
    for thee.
God keep our land
    glorious and free!
O Canada,
    we stand on guard for thee.
O Canada,
    we stand on guard for thee.

O Canada!
    Terre de nos aïeux,
Ton front est ceint
    de fleurons glorieux!
Car ton bras
    sait porter l'épée,
Il sait porter
    la croix!
Ton histoire
    est une épopée
Des plus
    brillants exploits.
Et ta valeur,
    de foi trempée,
Protégera nos foyers
    et nos droits,
Protégera nos foyers
    et nos droits.

THE ROYAL ANTHEM

God Save the Queen

God save our gracious Queen!
Long live our noble Queen!
God save the Queen!
Send her victorious,
Happy and glorious,
Long to reign over us.
God save the Queen!

JINGLE BELLS

Dashing through the snow
In a one-horse open sleigh;
O'er the fields we go,
Laughing all the way.
Bells on bob-tail ring,
Making spirits bright,
What fun it is to ride and sing
A sleighing song tonight.

Chorus:

Jingle Bells! Jingle Bells!
Jingle all the way!
Oh, what fun it is to ride in a one-horse open sleigh!
Oh! Jingle Bells! Jingle Bells!
Jingle all the way!
Oh, what fun it is to ride in a one-horse open sleigh!

Day or two ago
I thought I'd take a ride,
Soon Miss Fanny Bright was seated by my side,
The horse was lean and lank,
Misfortune seemed his lot,
He got into a drifted bank,
And we, we got upsot!

Chorus:

Jingle Bells! Jingle Bells!
Jingle all the way!
Oh, what fun it is to ride in a one-horse open sleigh!
Oh! Jingle Bells! Jingle Bells!
Jingle all the way!
Oh, what fun it is to ride in a one-horse open sleigh!

Now the ground is white,
Go it while you're young!
Take the girls tonight, and sing this sleighing song.
Just get bobtailed bay,
Two forty for his speed,
Then hitch him to an open sleigh
And crack! You'll take the lead.

Chorus:

Jingle Bells! Jingle Bells!
Jingle all the way!
Oh, what fun it is to ride in a one-horse open sleigh!
Oh! Jingle Bells! Jingle Bells!
Jingle all the way!
Oh, what fun it is to ride in a one-horse open sleigh!

NAMES/NICKNAMES

Notice that some men's and women's nicknames are the same or have the same pronunciation. Many nick names for children end in -y. Some names do not have nicknames. Add more names to the list.

MEN

Given Name	Nicknames
Albert	Al, Bert
Alexander	Alex, Al
Alfred	Al, Fred
Andrew	Andy, Drew
Anthony	Tony
Arnold	Arnie
Brian	_____
Christopher	Chris
Daniel	Dan, Danny
David	Dave, Davey
Edward	Ed, Eddie, Ted, Teddy
Elvis	_____
Eugene	Gene
Francis	Frank, Frankie
Franklin	Frank, Frankie
Gerald	Gerry, Jerry
James	Jim, Jimmy
John	Jack, Johnny
Joseph	Joe, Joey
Lawrence	Larry
Lee	_____
Louis	Lou, Louie
Mark	_____
Martin	Marty
Matthew	Matt, Matty
Melvin	Mel
Michael	Mike, Mikey
Nathaniel	Nat
Nicholas	Nick, Nicky
Patrick	Pat
Paul	_____
Peter	Pete, Petey
Richard	Dick, Rick, Rich, Ricky
Robert	Bob, Bobby, Rob, Robbie
Sean/Shawn	_____
Stephen	Steve, Stevie
Terrence	Terry
Thomas	Tom, Tommy
Theodore	Ted, Teddy
William	Bill, Will, Billy, Willy

WOMEN

Given Name	Nicknames
Ann, Anne	Annie
Barbara	Barb, Barbie
Carol, Carole	_____
Carolyn	_____
Catherine	Cathy
Christine	Christie, Tina, Chrissy, Chris
Cynthia	Cindy
Dorothy	Dot, Dottie
Elaine	_____
Emily	_____
Elizabeth	Beth, Betsy, Betty, Liz
Faith	_____
Fay, Faye	_____
Frances	Fran
Gloria	_____
Helen	_____
Hope	_____
Jacqueline	Jackie
Jane	_____
Janet	Jan
Jean, Jeanne	Jeannie
Jeanette	_____
Jessica	Jess, Jessie
Joan	Joannie
Joanne	Jo
Judith	Judy
Kathleen	Kathy
Linda	_____
Lisa	_____
Margaret	Peggy, Peg, Maggie
Margery	Marj
Martha	Marty
Mary	_____
Maryanne	_____
Patricia	Pat, Patty, Patsy
Roberta	Bobbie
Rose	Rosie
Sally	_____
Sandra	Sandy
Sharon	Sherry
Susan	Sue, Susie
Teresa	Terry

NATIONS/NATIONALITIES

Notice that many nationalities end in -ese, -ish, -an, -ian, or -i. Add more nations and nationalities to the list.

NATION	NATIONALITY	NATION	NATIONALITY
	(-ese)	Chile	**(-an)** Chilean
China	Chinese	Costa Rica	Costa Rican
Japan	Japanese	Cuba	Cuban
Lebanon	Lebanese	The Dominican	Dominican
Portugal	Portuguese	Republic	
Senegal	Senegalese	Germany	German
Sudan	Sudanese	Kenya	Kenyan
Vietnam	Vietnamese	Korea	Korean
_____	_____	Mexico	Mexican
_____	_____	Puerto Rico	Puerto Rican
		South Africa	South African
	(-ian)	Uganda	Ugandan
Argentina	Argentinian	United States	American
Australia	Australian	of America	
Brazil	Brazilian	Venezuela	Venezuelan
Canada	Canadian	_____	_____
Egypt	Egyptian	_____	_____
Ethiopia	Ethiopian		
Haiti	Haitian		**(-i)**
Hungary	Hungarian	Israel	Israeli
India	Indian	Kuwait	Kuwaiti
Indonesia	Indonesian	Pakistan	Pakistani
Iran	Iranian	Saudi Arabia	Saudi
Italy	Italian	Somalia	Somali
Nigeria	Nigerian	_____	_____
Panama	Panamanian	_____	_____
Peru	Peruvian		
Russia	Russian		**(irregular)**
_____	_____	France	French
_____	_____	Germany	German
		Greece	Greek
	(-ish)	Netherlands	Dutch
Denmark	Danish	Switzerland	Swiss
England	English	Thailand	Thai
Ireland	Irish	_____	_____
Poland	Polish	_____	_____
Spain	Spanish		
Sweden	Swedish		
Turkey	Turkish		
_____	_____		
_____	_____		

GOSSIP SECRETS

UNIT 5, PAGE 79: The Living Room

I love my living room. I stay in the living room all day. Sometimes I lie on the sofa and watch TV. Sometimes I listen to music and sleep in the armchair. Sometimes I walk on the coffee table and eat the plant there. I like to play with the pillow on the sofa and the lampshade on the lamp. I am a beautiful yellow cat.

UNIT 9, PAGE 173: Medical Problem

Last week a nineteen-year-old girl came to the hospital with her aunt. The girl was very weak and very tired. Her blood tests showed a problem, but she did not want treatment. Her religion was against medical treatment. The girl's aunt was angry. She said, "You must have treatment!" The girl said, "No. God will give me treatment." Then she and her aunt went away. They did not come back, so we don't know what happened.

UNIT 10, PAGE 199: School

In January, I started a computer course at a community college. The first class was very difficult. After class my car didn't start. It was snowing and cold. I was very unhappy. Fortunately, a student from my class helped me with my car. He helped me with the computer course, too. We studied together all semester. I got an "A" in the course, and next week we are getting married! What a wonderful semester!